CALAMITIES & CATASTROPHES
THE TEN ABSOLUTELY
WORST YEARS
IN HISTORY

DEREK WILSON

CALAMITIES & CATASTROPHES

THE TEN ABSOLUTELY WORST YEARS IN HISTORY

DEREK WILSON

MARBLE ARCH
PRESS

MARBLE ARCH PRESS

Marble Arch Press
1230 Avenue of the Americas
New York, NY 10020

First Marble Arch Press trade paperback edition December 2012

Marble Arch Press is a publishing collaboration between Short Books,
UK, and Atria Books, US.

Marble Arch Press and colophon are trademarks of Short Books.

For information about special discounts for bulk purchases, please contact Simon & Schuster Special Sales at 1-866-506-1949 or business@
simonandschuster.com

The Simon & Schuster Speakers Bureau can bring authors to your live
event. For more information or to book an event, contact the Simon
& Schuster Speakers Bureau at 1-866-248-3049 or visit our website at
www.simonspeakers.com.

Manufactured in the United States of America

10 9 8 7 6 5 4 3 2 1

Library of Congress Cataloging-in-Publication Data

ISBN 978-1-4767-1882-8
ISBN 978-1-4767-1884-2 (ebook)

Contents

Chapter One

541–2

Human societies may disintegrate for any one of a number of reasons – conquest, pestilence, internal strife or government incompetence. The tragedy which befell the civilisations of the Mediterranean world in 541–2 and undermined its two dominant empires was that all these woes fell upon them at the same time.

The empires in question were Rome and Persia. Both these mighty states could look back on a long and glorious past. They had increased their boundaries, built fine cities and established peace and firm government over their subject peoples. By the sixth century such achievements lay in a distant past, preserved only in imperial chronicles. But the tide of history had turned again – a fact that made the disasters of this year particularly poignant since they fell upon resurgent empires, empires that were just beginning to recover part of their former glory.

In the second century AD the Roman Empire had constituted a continuous band of territory from what is now Portugal to Iran. But, by the 520s, under pressure from 'barbarian' tribes from central Asia and northern Europe, its borders had shrunk to an area bordering the eastern Mediterranean from the Adriatic coast to the Nile valley. In fact, strictly speaking, it was no longer a *Roman* empire. The Emperor Constantine, who had ruled from 312 to 337, had made two major strategic decisions. He had moved his capital from Rome to Byzantium, on the Bosphorus, which he renamed Constantinople. The new centre was better placed for guarding the empire's Danube and Euphrates borders. He had also replaced a welter of pagan religions with one official religion – Christianity. This gave the heterogeneous empire a philosophical/political unity. Henceforth Christianity and classical culture would constitute the ideological foundation on which European civilisation was built.

The empire was stabilised under rule from two centres, Rome and Constantinople. However, when, in 527, Justinian I came to the throne, the civilisation was looking far from secure. What had been the Western Empire had become a patchwork of barbarian kingdoms – Visigoths ruled what is now Spain, Vandals controlled North Africa, Burgundians and Franks had divided between them what is modern France. Scandinavian and north

German tribes competed for Britain, and Ostrogoths were masters of Italy. The Eastern Roman Empire, usually called the Byzantine Empire was hard-pressed by Huns in the North and a revived Persian Empire in the East. In 540 a Bulgar army raided right up to the walls of Constantinople. And as if that wasn't bad enough, the Byzantine Empire itself was divided by competing versions of Christianity.

Seen against this background, the achievements of Justinian seem truly remarkable. He completely turned the tide of Byzantine affairs. If he had not had to face a variety of misfortunes which eventually proved to be overwhelming, he might well have restored the power and glory of ancient Rome. This emperor was as forceful and ruthless as he was intelligent. There was no area of life on which he did not set his stamp. After the Bulgar raid he completely rebuilt the fortifications along the northern border. He recodified the laws. He imposed uniformity on the feuding religious factions and made himself the supreme authority in Church as well as state. He outlawed heretics and homosexuals. He forced through administrative and financial reforms, improved the defensive fortifications of the empire and built several churches. The material symbol of his greatness can still be seen in the magnificent Church of Santa Sophia (now a mosque), with its huge dome, which still crowns the skyline of Constantinople (now named Istanbul).

Establishing strong government after years of corruption and administrative incompetence called for ruthlessness. The emperor was hard and uncompromising and he was aided in his reforming programme by some powerful advisers and agents. Foremost among them was his wife, the Empress Theodora. Theodora is one of the most extraordinary women in all of ancient history, and certainly the most important in the story of the Byzantine Empire. Before Justinian made her his mistress and later, his wife, she had been an actress and a woman of very dubious morality. But she was mentally strong and highly intelligent. She came to exercise considerable power and even had a pope deposed on her sole authority. Justinian relied heavily on her advice and she was at her best in times of crisis. On many occasions, the emperor would have abandoned his plans in the light of strong opposition had not Theodora provided an example of unflinching leadership.

Justinian was also fortunate in having in his service a talented administrator and legal adviser: John the Cappadocian. John was a born bureaucrat with a clear mind unclouded by compassion or human sympathy. Justinian's reforms would have been quite impossible without an administrator as single-minded as he was himself. It was John who helped to draw up the new legal code, and he imposed it without fear or favour. Justinian appointed him praetorian prefect of the Eastern Empire, with widespread powers to levy taxes and oversee regional governments. John weeded out ineffective officials and men who were using their office to amass personal fortunes. As far as possible he replaced them with others chosen on merit. He was not afraid to stand up to the emperor or to attempt to dissuade him from policies such as foreign wars, which would deplete the treasury and divert funds from administrative reconstruction. Inevitably, his draconian measures aroused opposition. This diatribe by one of his enemies indicates how much he was hated:

…the villainous John the Cappadocian… proceeded to cause misfortunes that were felt by the general public. First, he set out chains and shackles, stocks and irons. Within the praetor's court he established a private prison there in the darkness for punishments that were inflicted upon those who came under his authority… There he shut up those who were being subject to restraint. He exempted no one, whatever his station, from torture. He has no compunction about stringing up, without holding an enquiry, those among whom the only information that had been laid was that they possessed gold… they were either stripped of all they possessed or dead before he let them go… A certain Antiochus, who was advanced in years at the time when this happened, was named by an informer who told a tale to John that he possessed some gold. So John arrested him and strung him up by the hands, which were fastened by strong, fine cords, until the old man, who denied the charge, was a corpse.

Justinian's reign coincided with that of another great ruler in Persia. Khusro I (sometimes spelled Chosroes), who ruled from 531 to 579, was the most outstanding king of the Sassanid dynasty. The Sassanian Empire, founded in 221, had, at its apogee, extended from what is now Turkey to Pakistan and from the Caspian Sea to both shores of the Persian Gulf. However, like the Roman Empire, it had passed its peak by the early sixth century. Enter Khusro I. He was, in many ways, similar to Justinian – forceful and ruthless, an administrative reformer and a builder who left behind several new palaces, fortifications and even towns. Khusro presided over a cultural renaissance. A Christian chronicler, John of Ephesus, wrote of him:

> He was a prudent and wise man, and all his lifetime took pains to collect the religious books of all creeds, and read and study them, that he might learn which were true and wise and which were foolish.

Under Khusro, Sassanian art reached its peak of achievement. Everything from clay seals, silverware, pottery and glass to monumental palace architecture testified to the aesthetic refinement, wealth and power of the dynasty. When pagan philosophers were expelled from Athens, Khusro welcomed them to his own capital of Ctesiphon, a city as grand as Constantinople, but now vanished. At the same time he introduced from India the game of chess.

Khusro's political problems mirrored those of Justinian. His empire was beset by internal sectarian divisions within the national religion of Zoroastrianism and by political revolts. Persia faced the constant threat of Huns along its extended northern and eastern frontiers. In 484 they had ravaged the eastern half of the empire and slaughtered a whole Sassanid army, led by the Persian king. Khusro spent the early years of his reign concentrating on overhauling the tax system and imposing long-overdue military reforms. One of his first acts was to agree with Justinian a treaty of 'Endless Peace'. No less than Justinian, the Persian king needed to avoid distractions while he dealt with the empire's internal problems and while he secured his eastern frontier. But, again like Justinian, Khusro was a ruler with huge ambitions. His aim was nothing less than to obtain a stranglehold over all the land and sea routes along which flowed the precious cargoes of merchandise from India and China. Thus, while it was in the interests of both empires to put an end to their rivalry, such a respite could only be temporary.

One reason Justinian was pleased to be free of distractions in the East was his determination on territorial expansion in the West. His ambitions went far beyond establishing strong and efficient government in the Byzantine East. He had never accepted the loss of the western provinces and he was determined to bring together the two halves of the ancient Roman Empire. In this he was assisted by another talented servant, Belisarius. Belisarius was one of the great generals of antiquity, as imaginative and cunning as he was merciless. He also had the advantage of being married to a lady called Antonina, who was a close friend of Theodora. The first test of his loyalty and ability came in 532, when John the Cappadocian's reforms sparked the first internal crisis of the reign. A revolt blew up in Constantinople and its leaders demanded the sacrifice of the most eminent imperial administrators. Some called for the deposition of the emperor. Justinian would have fled the capital had it not been for the steadfast example of Theodora. She called upon the services of Belisarius and he put a swift and bloody end to the insurrection. He hoodwinked the rebels into a meeting in the hippodrome, ostensibly to present their grievances. Once he had them inside the arena, Belisarius had the entrances sealed and sent in his troops. According to contemporary accounts, 30,000 rebels were massacred that day. Thereafter, Justinian was free from internal discord.

Justinian now employed Belisarius to carry out his reconquest of the western half of the old empire. In a series of brilliant campaigns between 533 and 535, Belisarius crushed the Vandals and captured their capital of Carthage. North Africa was reconquered for the Roman Empire. The following year, Belisarius crossed the sea, occupied Sicily, then moved northwards through Italy, reaching the city of Ravenna in 540, where he captured the Ostrogoth king and sent him back to Constantinople in chains. Justinian was not best pleased with this humiliation of his enemy. According to his political calculation, the stability of the empire would have been better served by allowing the Ostrogoths to rule a client kingdom in North Italy, paying tribute to Constantinople, until Byzantine rule in the peninsula had been firmly established. The emperor wanted a friendly buffer state to protect his own territory against the Franks to the North. Nevertheless, this turning of the tide of history was a remarkable achievement and just might have led to the re-establishment of Roman rule through the Mediterranean if Byzantium had not been beset by a clutch of new problems.

Justinian had scarcely received the news of victory over the barbarians in the West when he heard of a crisis on the eastern frontier. The Persian king Khusro, urged on by the Ostrogoths, who wanted the Romans to divert their forces from Italy, decided that now was the moment to have a go at attacking Byzantium. The temptation was too. By now he had energetically addressed his domestic problems, reorganised his army and was ready to confront the old enemy. So it was that, in 540, the two great empires once more went to war. Khusro marched through Syria, captured several Byzantine towns and made for the great prize of Antioch, one of the richest trading centres in Justinian's realm. Antioch, as Khusro knew, was vulnerable. Although it had stout walls, they had recently been severely damaged by an earthquake. The citizens were unable to prevent the Persians looting and burning their city and carrying off thousands of its inhabitants into slavery. Khusro settled them in a newly built town which he called 'Khusro's-Better-than-Antioch'. Emboldened by easy victory, he then pressed home his advantage. In the next year's campaign he headed for the Black Sea province of Lazika (part of modern Georgia). Justinian sent Belisarius to repel the resurgent Persians and the region was subjected to months of raid and counter-raid.

For Justinian, the campaigns in North Africa, Italy and Lazika were ruinously expensive. He had inherited a full treasury but, by 541, it was virtually empty. What the emperor needed was a few years of peace in which to establish imperial administration in his newly won territories, so that, from taxes and the increase of trade, he could recoup the money expended in conquest. Khusro, too, would have benefited from a period in which to consolidate his gains. What neither ruler reckoned with was the appearance of a new enemy which would make a mockery of both of their calculations – bubonic plague.

This new disaster, which fell upon both great empires, and put their problems into a new perspective, was the outcome of a set of circumstances that had probably begun in 536. Severe meteorological disturbances occurred over the greater part of the northern hemisphere. Procopius, the contemporary Palestinian historian of the Roman Empire, recorded: 'a most dread portent took place... the sun gave forth its light without brightness... the beams it shed were not clear.' Instances of excessively low temperatures, crop failures and drought were recorded in Ireland, China, Peru and Europe. A devastating event affected life in Scandinavia, North America and Greenland. Over a vast area the light of the sun was filtered through a dust cloud, resulting in dramatic falls in temperature. There could be no contemporary explanation for these phenomena, but recent scientific speculation has come up with two possible causes. Some suggest that the dust cloud was the result of volcanic activity. Cataclysmic eruptions (though on a smaller scale) in recent centuries have spewed thousands of tons of sulphur dioxide into the atmosphere, giving rise to 'dry fog' and acid rain, which have been disastrous for crops, animals and humans. Could the Indonesian volcano, Krakatoa, have been responsible for a veil which spread around the globe? The other possible cause is comet activity. Meterorite bombardment has long been suggested as a possible cause for the climatic change that brought to an end the age of dinosaurs. A large piece of debris from a comet tail striking the earth at several thousand kph. would have a force equivalent to over 1,000 atomic bombs and would throw up a plume of dust which would rapidly spread through the atmosphere and take months or years to disperse. One theory states that just such a dramatic event occurred in northern Australia in 536.

Whatever happened at that time was the result of the most destructive force to hit our planet in thousands of years; the effect on the climate was profound, with disastrous consquences for the ecological balance. Hitherto, plague had been confined to the tropical regions of Africa. The rat parasite that carries bubonic plague can only flourish at moderate temperatures. The heat of the desert and semi-desert band that crosses the continent from modern Senegal to Sudan was a barrier

it could not cross. The temperature drop caused
by the dust cloud breached that northern African
barrier long enough for the fleas to cross into the
temperate Mediterranean zone. Procopius charted
its spread:

> It started from the Egyptians who dwell in Pelusium
> [near modern Port Said]. Then it divided and moved
> in one direction towards Alexandria and the rest of
> Egypt, and in the other direction it came to Palestine
> on the borders of Egypt; and from there it spread
> over the whole world, always moving forward and
> travelling at times favourable to it. For it seemed to
> move by fixed arrangement, and to tarry for a speci-
> fied time in each country, casting its blight slight-
> ingly upon none, but spreading in either direction
> right out to the ends of the world, as if fearing lest
> some corner of the earth might escape it.

Alexandria was a great mercantile entrepôt in
the sixth century. In its waterfront warehouses
the produce of North Africa, 'the granary of the
Roman Empire', was stored. It was the terminus of
vital trade routes which avoided Persian territory
and brought, by sea and overland caravan, African
slaves, Chinese silks, Indian gems and Indonesian
spices. Large fleets regularly plied across the eastern
Mediterranean to Constantinople. By 541 they
were carrying a new and unwelcome cargo.

Today, we can describe clinically the symptoms of bubonic plague and how it spreads. The rat flea carries a bacterium, *Y. pestis*. As the rat moves through unsanitary and crowded towns and villages, the flea 'jumps ship', seeking a new host – animal or human. When the flea bites its latest victim, the bacterium, which does not harm the rat, is transferred to its new body, with disastrous results. Once in the bloodstream, *Y. pestis* makes its way to the lymph glands, which swell and rupture, appearing on the surface as painful, dark-coloured 'buboes' in the groin or armpits. The victim falls prey to shivering, fever and stiffening of the joints. He/she may experience delirium or fall into a coma. Once the lungs are infected, the plague takes on a new form – pneumonic. Miniscule droplets of sputum are exhaled with every breath, carrying the plague to new victims. The original sufferer has become a machine gun of highly infectious bullets. For several days the newly infected victims display no symptoms. The plague is, therefore, hidden; its real impact concealed. Half of the people catching bubonic plague, if they were reasonably fit and healthy beforehand, survive. Pneumonic plague is virtually one hundred per cent fatal.

It was not only the disease itself that killed people. Some, in delirium or sheer desperation, took their own lives. Some starved to death because there was no one to bring them food. Understandably, neighbours avoided houses where plague victims were lying. More compassionate people faced hardship caring for the afflicted, even if they did not contract the disease:

> ...when patients fell from their beds and lay rolling on the floor, they kept putting them back in place, and when they were struggling to rush headlong out of their houses, they would force them back by shoving and pulling against them. And when water chance to be near [the sufferers] wished to fall into it... because of... the diseased state of their minds.

People took to wearing name tags, so that they could be identified in the event of sudden death. The forums and public places were deserted.

> At that time it was scarcely possible to meet anyone going about the streets of Byzantium; all who had the good fortune to be in health were sitting in their houses, either attending the sick or mourning the dead. If one did succeed in encountering a man going out, he was carrying one of the dead. And work of every description ceased, and all the trades were abandoned by the artisans... Indeed in a city which was simply abounding in all good things widespread starvation was running riot... so that with some of the sick it appeared that the end of life

came about sooner than it should have because they lacked the necessities of life.

Fifteen hundred years ago, observers lacked the knowledge of human anatomy and epidemiology that would have enabled them to describe the pestilence objectively. Such medical science as they possessed was freely mixed with religious belief and superstition. Chroniclers, appalled by what they saw and fearful of what it might mean, prophesied the utter destruction of the empire, or even of the entire human race. They readily reported portents in the heavens warning of imminent disaster. They passed on stories of visions and mystical experiences:

> ...many people saw shapes of bronze boats carrying passengers with their heads cut off... These figures were seen everywhere as frightening manifestations, especially at night. They appeared like gleaming bronze and fire, black and without heads they sat in their glistening boats, travelling rapidly across the water – a sight which made those who saw it almost drop dead.

Both the Byzantine and Persian empires possessed physicians and philosopher/astrologers whose understanding of the human condition was advanced by the standards of the day, but they were powerless to cope with this new and terrible visitation. The second-century physician, Galen, whose thinking had dominated medical theory and practice for centuries, made important discoveries about the nervous system and the 'flow' (not circulation) of blood, but his assertion that health was determined by the balance of four 'humours' which had their bases in blood, phlegm, black bile and yellow bile was of no value in combating plague. His disciples sought to achieve 'balance' in their patients by a combination of simple drugs, incantations, the application of saints' bones and other magical charms, diet and exercise. The only result of such clinical methods was that many doctors succumbed to plague as a result of close contact with their patients. Small wonder that Procopius was sceptical about the medical services available:

> ...the most illustrious physicians predicted that many would die, who unexpectedly escaped entirely from suffering... and declared that many would be saved, who were destined to be carried off almost immediately.

Potentially more valuable was the practice of isolating plague victims. Hospitals were the invention of early Christians in Palestine and, by the fifth century, they were to be found in many towns and cities of the Roman Empire. There were several in Constantinople, and Justinian provided state aid to them to cope with the new emergency, but these institutions were soon overwhelmed by the sheer size of the problem. Procopius and other chroniclers have left us a vivid and horrifying picture of life in the Byzantine capital during these dreadful months, and the scenes they recorded must have been replicated in other towns and cities.

The most urgent problem was disposal of the dead. The city's cemeteries were soon filled, even when people were being buried three or more to a grave. Justinian commandeered waste or unused land to provide more burial grounds but these, too, were overflowing within weeks. The next location found for cadavers was along the city walls. At regular intervals there were watchtowers, designed to house soldiers to man the walls when Constantinople came under attack. These empty buildings were now used for a more gruesome purpose. Their roofs were removed and bodies were thrown inside and stamped on in order to get as many as possible into the space available. The stench drifting over the city was appalling. The terrible reality presents a real challenge to the imagination, as another contemporary writer bewailed:

How can anyone speak of or recount such a hideous sight, and who can watch this burial, even though his soul remain in his body and not waste away from bitter lamentations over so much iniquity which would suffice to destroy the children of Adam? How and with what utterances and what hymns, with what funeral laments and groanings should somebody mourn who has survived and witnessed the wine-press of the fury of the wrath of God?

There is no way of knowing exactly how many people died in the East Roman capital during this terrible visitation, but contemporaries claimed that between a third and a half of Constantinople's citizens succumbed and that this degree of mortality was replicated throughout the Eastern Roman Empire. The plague had no respect; it claimed victims at all levels of society. The emperor himself caught the disease. He was one of the lucky ones not to die but he was ill for several weeks. Had it not been for the vigorous efforts of the Empress Theodora and a small team of palace officials, the running of the empire might well have collapsed in chaos. While the emperor remained incapacitated, officials looked to Theodora for instructions, and it was she who masterminded the provision of aid to sufferers and maintained some semblance of law and order. John the Cappadocian was no longer there to apply his considerable administrative skills to overcoming the crisis. He had survived the mounting tide of criticism, but he could not surmount the opposition of Theodora. The empress was increasingly jealous of John's influence with her husband and eventually she had him stripped of office and sent into exile. Almost at once the Byzantine bureaucracy began to slip back into corruption and was quite unable to handle the effects of plague.

Death brought other grave problems in its wake. Because of the threat of invasion, Justinian had made sure that Constantinople's grain stores were full. But there were soon few bakers left to make bread, and those that were still in business charged inflated prices. There was famine in the midst of plenty and malnutrition kept pestilence company on the streets. The economic effects were no less disastrous than the loss of life. Slavery was the basis of Byzantine society and when the stock of slaves was drastically cut, all human activities were affected. Farm animals went untended. Shops remained closed. Businesses went out of production. Ships rotted in harbour for want of mariners to sail them and chandlers to equip them. Aristocratic households could not function without indoor and outdoor servants. The army was severely depleted. Government business came to a standstill. Inevitably, the costs of labour and goods rocketed, resulting in rapid inflation. In a desperate attempt to stabilise the currency, the coinage was debased. This made matters worse since those who could afford to do so hoarded gold and silver, which drove down the value of coin, forcing producers to charge more for their goods and workers to demand higher wages. The government tried to halt the wage-price spiral by forbidding workers to raise the price of their labour. In March 544, Justinian issued the following edict:

> Pursuant to the chastening that we have received in the benevolence of our Lord God, some people... have abandoned themselves to avarice and demand double and triple prices and wages that are contrary to the custom prevalent from antiquity, although such people ought rather to have been chastened by this calamity. It is therefore our decision to forbid such covetous greed... In the future no businessman, workman or artisan in any occupation, trade, or agricultural pursuit shall dare to charge a higher price or wage than that of the custom prevalent from antiquity.

It is no surprise that this clumsy attempt to frustrate the laws of simple economics had little effect.

Inevitably, fear and grief drove people to ask the question: 'Why?' Procopius confessed himself baffled:

> Now in the case of all other scourges sent from heaven some explanation of a cause might be

given by daring men, such as the many theories propounded by those who are clever in these matters, for they love to conjure up causes which are absolutely incomprehensible to man... but for this calamity, it is quite impossible either to express in words or to conceive in thought any explanation, except indeed to refer it to God.

Later moralists, who saw the events of the 540s as precursors to the collapse of the Sassanian and Western Roman empires, had less hesitation. A seventh-century monastic chronicler interpreted the catastrophe in terms of divine judgement. God had sent his agents to punish the arrogant presumption and cruelties of the ancient empires:

The land of the Persian was given to Devastation for him to devastate it, sending its inhabitants to captivity and to slaughter: Syria was given to the sword of Devastation, its inhabitants to captivity and to slaughter; the Roman empire was given to Devastation and its inhabitants to captivity and to slaughter.

By the time this writer recorded his view of history, he was able to see the plague as part of the long-term decline of Sassanian Persia and of Rome's empire in the West. To those who lived through these terrible times, matters were more complex.

The enemies of the Byzantine Empire were not slow to take advantage of its weakness. The Persians attempted to press home their advantage in the region between the Black Sea and Mesopotamia and laid siege to Edessa. The inconclusive war went on for months and ended in a truce under whose terms Khusro undertook to remove his troops from the area for five years, in return for a payment of 2,000 pounds in gold. It was a heavy price, but Justinian needed to buy time. Affairs were going badly in Italy. Under a new king, the Ostrogoths were mounting a fresh offensive, steadily reclaiming territory which the Byzantines had gained. Justinian had to send Belisarius back to the West in a desperate attempt to cling onto his conquests there. But the great general was woefully short of resources. The plague had decimated the Byzantine army and economic difficulties created shortages of equipment. Belisarius found himself bogged down in a long and, eventually, unsuccessful series of campaigns. The grand vision of recreating the glories of the Roman Empire had to be abandoned.

The debilitating effects of the plague cannot be described only in terms of economic and political decline. There was a widespread sense of fatalism. When Bulgars and other tribes displaced by the Huns raided into the Balkans and northern Greece, they encountered little resistance. The garrisons that should have defended the inhabitants were seriously undermanned and the people had no confidence in the government to protect them. They had to suffer the barbarian incursions, watch their homes being pillaged and their womenfolk raped. There was only one way to put an end to their ordeal: they had to pay the invaders to go away. Some wealthy citizens hid their treasures – and many never returned to reclaim them. Numerous hoards of buried coins, silver plate and gold ornaments have been found throughout this region – graphic testimony to the turbulence of the times. Administration broke down and much of Justinian's reforming work was undone.

Yet, ironically, the pestilence thaht devastated the Eastern Roman Empire also saved it from more severe depredations. The plague took no account of territorial boundaries, as Procopius recorded:

> ...this calamity... did not come in one part of the world or upon certain men, nor did it confine itself to any season of the year, so that from such circumstances it might be possible to find subtle explanations of a cause, but it embraced the entire world, and blighted the lives of all men, though differing from one another in the most marked degree, respecting neither sex nor age.

When he described this catastrophe as one that 'embraced the entire world', Procopius was, of course, referring to the world he knew: Europe, the Middle East, northern Africa and the nearer parts of Asia. However, this outbreak reached well beyond the fringes of the known Mediterranean world and resulted in human mortality on an unimaginable and incalculable scale. It galloped over mountains, deserts and seas, striking down men, women and children as far away as Ireland, China and the African interior.

Thus, for example, raiders across the borders of the weakened Byzantine Empire often took back with them more than sackfuls of loot. When the Alemanni (a Germanic tribe) leader, Leutharis, led a raid into northern Italy, he was able to plunder at will but, when he turned for home with his laden wagons of loot,

> He became deranged and started raving like a madman. [He] was seized with a violent ague and would fall over backwards, foaming at the mouth, his eyes glaring dreadfully... The plague continued to rage until his whole army was destroyed.

Unfortunately, no Persian records describing events in the 540s have survived, but Byzantine writers recorded, in brief, the spread of contagion into the territory of the invader. John of Ephesus referred to this period in Persia's history as years of 'famine, plague, madness and fury'. Khusro had to give up the siege of Edessa when many of his troops succumbed to disease. *Y. pestis* travelled with Khusro's armies and along his trade routes. Antioch, Nisibis and other important centres were virtually depopulated. Khusro, victorious over his human enemies and confident of further military successes, had encountered a foe he could not beat. It was Persian weakness, not Byzantine strength, that prevented Persia advancing irresistibly westwards. Militarily, the mid-540s were years of stagnation. Two mighty empires stood like punch-drunk boxers, eyeing each other blearily, swaying from side to side and unable to land any telling blows.

Matters were little different in Europe, beyond the farthest Byzantine borders. The plague is recorded as reaching Frankish territory in 543. Familiar, dreadful scenes were soon to be witnessed throughout Gaul (the land of the Franks):

> …so many people were killed throughout the whole region and the dead bodies were so numerous that it was not even possible to count them. There was such a shortage of coffins and tombstones that ten or more bodies were buried in the same grave. In St Peter's church [in Clermont-Ferrand] alone on a single Sunday three hundred dead bodies were counted. Death came very quickly. An open sore like a snake's bite appeared in the groin or the armpit,

and the man who had it soon died of its poison, breathing his last on the second or third day.

In terms of the long haul of history, the real impact of plague and war in the years 541–2 was on the size of populations. In the twenty-first century we face the problem of overpopulation. Fifteen hundred years ago societies that felt themselves just as secure as we do fell into the abyss of drastic population collapse. In the first two years of the pandemic it has been suggested that four million of the East Roman Empire's twenty-six million inhabitants disappeared and the decline continued as *Y. pestis* sought out more victims. Whole villages and towns vanished. Cities shrank. Crumbling walls left their citizens vulnerable to marauders. Farmland fell into disuse. Governments faced declining revenue and could no longer provide their people with the benefits of advanced civilisation. The same phenomena were to be observed in Persia and the other nations fringing the Mediterranean world.

These ancient societies were not allowed time to recover. Long before population levels, stable government and a measure of prosperity had returned, the Persians and Byzantines faced another foe. Within a century, the great civilisations that had shared the world of the Mediterranean basin found themselves facing a new, vigorous, expanding empire, bursting out of its Arabian heartland. Less than thirty years after the plague visitation of Constantinople, a boy was born in Mecca whose impact upon the lands where Christianity and Zoroastrianism flourished would, in its way, be as devastating as the earlier rat-borne invasion. His name was Mohammed. When the armies of Islam marched out of Arabia carrying their new faith, at swordpoint, to all points of the compass, the older civilisations had been so weakened that they had no effective answer.

The circumstances under which the ancient Mediterranean civilisations collapsed present us with several 'what ifs'. What if court rivalries had not forced John the Cappadocian from office? What if Theodora had lived longer (she died in 548)? What if Justinian and Khusro had managed to agree a lasting peace? What if the bubonic plague had not struck when it did? These lead us to bigger questions. Could the empire of Rome have been recreated in the sixth century? Could the Sassanian and Roman empires have survived barbarian incursions? Impressive ancient ruins litter the lands from Spain's Atlantic coast to the River Indus. Valley-spanning viaducts, soaring pillars that once graced temples, wide amphitheatres scooped from the earth, the crumbling walls of beautiful palaces, javelin-straight highways along which the legions once marched – all such examples of vanished grandeur stir us to wonder and to reflect on the reasons why empires rise and fall.

Chapter 2

1241–2

The Mongol Empire was the largest empire of all time; larger, in fact, than all the world's other major empires put together. From their base in the region of Karakorum – east of the modern city of Ulaanbaatar in modern Mongolia – these remarkable nomadic warriors conquered many of the peoples of the Eurasian land mass and, with no sophisticated administrative system, held sway over a domain extending from the German frontier to Korea, and from the Arctic Ocean to the Persian Gulf. They even made seaborne assaults on Japan and Java. The Mongols came to rule most of the world that existed – as far as they knew. They clashed with older and technically more advanced civilisations in what are now China, Tibet, Russia, Poland, Bulgaria, Iran, Iraq, Turkey, Hungary, Georgia, Armenia and Palestine. They incorporated in their empire devotees of three major religions – Christianity, Islam and Buddhism. But what they tolerated was vastly outweighed by what they rejected and overthrew. Farmland was torched, towns and cities were left as smouldering ruins. Whole peoples were uprooted and driven before the invaders, some obliged to become conquerors in their turn, in their quest for living space. They enjoyed a well-earned reputation for military might, bravery and violence. They wrought havoc wherever they went and struck fear into the hearts of all who lay in the path of their irrepressible expansion.

The Mongols found such success not because they *had* a great army, but because they *were* a great army. Reared on the poor grassland of the steppes, where grazing was sparse, these people had to be constantly on the move, searching for pasture and, when necessary, driving off the existing inhabitants. They lived on horseback and were masters at handling their small, sturdy ponies, which had as much stamina as their riders. The Mongols hunted with bow and arrow from horseback. They were, in effect – and were reared from childhood to be – a light cavalry. Theirs was a military culture. Their warrior bands possessed endurance, mobility and discipline. When other civilisations that had developed the arts of warfare in their own ways – perfecting armour, weapons and fortifications to suit their own needs – confronted these simply-accoutred fighting units, they were at a loss to know how to deal with them. This largely accounts for the devastation the Mongols wrought when they fell upon the armies of armoured knights who were the cream of medieval European society. The shock inflicted by the invaders in 1241–2 was as great as the devastation they caused. Outlandish, fearless, fearsome, these 'devils' threatened to put an end to a millennium of Christian civilisation and to sweep all before them until they reached the Atlantic. However, boldness and brutality alone would not have turned fighters into conquerors. What made the difference was the emergence among them of leaders who were master strategists and tacticians.

The greatest of them was Temujin, who, in 1206, brought all the tribes under his control and was thenceforth known as Genghis Khan, or 'universal ruler'. We would today label him a psychopathic monster and recognise in him characteristics that have marked other dictators: he had an obsessive belief in his divine mission to rule the world. He was not restricted by any moral scruples in the pursuance of his vision, and he demanded from all and every one of his people unquestioning loyalty. But he was no fool; quite the contrary. He based his campaigns on carefully gathered intelligence and executed them with imagination and cunning. In 1211 he began his invasion of the Chin Empire of northern China. Three armies breached the Great Wall and attacked towns and cities lying along the route of their southward march. Genghis learned from his enemies the arts of siege warfare and used captives to build siege engines to destroy their own defences. He also forced captives to march in front of his own forces in order to face the missiles of the defenders. These were formidable indeed. Sophisticated Chin weapons included crossbows capable of launching arrows 500 metres, wagon-mounted catapults, gunpowder missiles and flaming naphtha. Genghis Khan collected information about all these unfamiliar techniques. Khanbalik (modern Beijing), formerly considered impregnable, fell in 1215 after a year-long siege. Prisoners were of value only as sources of information, forced labour or 'cannon fodder'. The war against the ancient Chinese civilisations continued for seventy years – long after Genghis Khan's death (1227). But there was no stopping the impetus to conquest which he had begun. In 1235 the Mongols turned their attention to Europe.

Thirteenth-century Europe was a region with twin identities. From the secular viewpoint it was a conglomeration of feudal states whose rulers were frequently in competition with each other for territorial or economic gain. All central Europe, from the Rhine valley to Vienna and from the Baltic coast to central Italy, constituted the German Empire. Scores of semi-autonomous principalities, dukedoms and archdioceses lay under the overall rule of the Holy Roman Emperor. But these states, together with the rest of the continent, also had a common religious identity. They were Latin Christendom, under the spiritual rule of the pope in Rome. Church and state were closely intertwined. Because the rulers of Christian Europe were often at war among themselves, military training was an integral part of social life. The art and science of European warfare rested on two foundations: the castle and the knight. Kings and nobles dominated their lands and defended themselves within massive fortifications which, by the thirteenth century, had reached a high degree of sophistication. Much of medieval warfare centred on the siege, the attempt to storm or starve into submission the castle garrisons.

When a great man went forth to battle, the cream of his army was the mounted knight. This warrior rode a large, powerful horse, encased his body in chain mail or plate armour, wore a helmet sometimes surmounted by a crest or plume, carried a shield proudly blazoned with his personal heraldic device and sported an array of weapons, prominent among which were the lance and broadsword. The charge of a massed body of knights was intended to and often did strike fear into the enemy. Once the adversaries' battle line had been broken, cavalry and supporting infantry engaged in hand-to-hand fighting.

Knighthood was surrounded by a pseudo-religious mystique known as the code of chivalry. Bards, minstrels and troubadours sang songs and told tales of brave and saintly deeds performed by such heroes as the legendary King Arthur. For two centuries and more this military culture had dominated western warfare and had never been confronted with a rival culture with different values and ways of fighting. That was about to change.

Ogodei Khan, who succeeded his father Genghis Khan as Mongol overlord in 1229, was determined to widen the borders of the territory he had inherited from his father. He summoned a military council at Karakorum in 1235 to plan a grand strategy. Batu, Ogodei's nephew, was allocated the westward advance, which he was to undertake in conjunction with the veteran general, Subedei. Their immediate targets were to be Russian princes, whose territories lay south of the Baltic, and the peoples of the Hungarian plain. The Mongols had some knowledge of these potential victims but beyond lay unknown lands, said to be phenomenally wealthy and offering enticing prospects of considerable booty. In 1236 an enormous dust cloud moved across central and western Asia, raised by more than 100,000 horsemen. News of this terrifying military juggernaut reached Vienna, Rome, Paris and London – and was dismissed as ludicrous exaggeration. As the Bishop of Winchester remarked casually, if these barbarians are on the move, what concern is that of Christian civilisation: 'Let us leave these dogs to devour one another.'

In Russia the approach of a large army did not provoke undue dismay because the towns and cities of the region were protected by dense forest, which would slow down and dissipate the Mongol horde. What a shock it was to hear that the invaders were hacking wide swathes through the trees and advancing steadily with carts carrying siege engines. The princes had not combined their forces to confront the threat and their settlements fell, one after another. The merciless slaughter and destruction were on an epic scale. It was a Mongol custom to keep a tally of their victims by cutting an ear from each enemy corpse. By the time they had finished with the Russians, their haul amounted to 270,000 ears.

While his warriors moved into winter quarters to divide up their loot, Batu sent spies ahead into Europe to gather information in preparation for his next campaigns. He also despatched envoys to King Béla IV of Hungary and Pope Gregory IX, demanding unconditional surrender. Béla did call on the emperor for support but Gregory, who considered himself to be God's viceroy in ruling the entire universe, paid no attention to threats from what one theologian called 'the detestable people of Satan'.

Rome was far enough away to be safe. The same was not true of the capital of Russian Orthodox Christianity, Kiev. Russia's grandest city boasted a magnificent cathedral and 400 churches. When the Mongols surrounded it in 1240, it must have seemed that the maw of hell had belched forth a demonic pestilence against the people of God. As the invaders encircled it, one chronicler described the fear of the intimidated citizenry: 'The rattling of their innumerable carts, the bellowing of camels and cattle, the neighing of horses and the wild battle cries were so overwhelming as to render inaudible conversation within the city.' Kiev was utterly destroyed and never regained its former ascendancy.

In the winter of 1241 Batu's marauders crossed the frozen Ukrainian grasslands towards Poland, the last barrier to central Europe. Lublin fell to them, then Cracow. The people of Wroclau fled to safety, leaving their homes in flames rather than allowing the Mongols to violate them. The great city of Breslau successfully resisted and, instead of wasting the advantage of their impetus in a long siege, the Mongols passed it by. Now it was clear that these savages would have to be faced with a superior force of the world's finest mounted warriors: the Christian knights. Among the European elite there was no doubt that their iron-clad champions would wipe the floor with the wild-eyed nomads from the uncivilised wastes of the Asian steppes. So, at last, national leaders girded themselves to defend Christian culture.

The enemy they so seriously underestimated was as clever as he was violent. Subedei's strategy would stand up to comparison with that of Caesar,

Napoleon or any other great Western general. In 1241 his smashing of Poland was a massive diversionary tactic to draw potential enemy forces away from his principal objective, Hungary. Subedei divided his host into three armies. A northern wing of 20,000 men was committed to the advance through Poland and started out first. He was kept fully informed of the progress of his men by an extremely efficient pony express service. The post riders covered long distances through difficult enemy country at remarkable speed so that the commander-in-chief had news of significant events within hours. After two weeks, when he knew how successful the assault on Poland had been, Subedei launched the rest of his horde. Subedei led the main army of some 30,000 warriors directly into Hungary, while a smaller contingent was despatched across the Carpathian mountains to ensure that the Mongols would not be surprised by an attack on their southern flank.

Why were Batu and Subedei particularly intent on the conquest of Hungary? The basic answer was that it was an easy target offering rich pickings. Hungary was the leading state of south-western Europe, boasting fine cities, churches, cathedrals and the well-filled houses of nobles and merchants. Mongol chiefs needed constant victories. Their support depended on keeping their followers supplied with booty. Any ruler who settled for an easy life, enjoying the fruits of earlier successes, would not remain ruler for long. Mongol expansionism generated its own momentum. Conquest was the only necessary justification. But Batu had, or claimed to have, specific grievances with the Hungarians. In earlier conflicts Mongols had clashed with another nomadic tribe, the Cumans. They had fled, en masse, into Hungary and had been given asylum to settle on the plains. Batu demanded the return of his 'servants' and warned Béla that failure to comply would be severely punished. The Cumans, he observed, lived in tents and would find escape relatively easy, but the soft Hungarian city-dwellers would be like sitting ducks to his warriors. Béla not only failed to heed this warning, he also murdered the envoys. Honour and revenge demanded that King Béla and his people should pay a heavy price for their 'treachery'. The Cumans might have been a considerable asset to the Hungarians in their forthcoming conflict. They were experts in the kind of fast-moving, versatile battle tactics at which the Mongols excelled. Unfortunately, internal rivalries deprived Béla of their services. A rumour was circulated that the Cumans were secretly allied to the Mongols and were only waiting for their moment to turn on their hosts. This was the kind of misunderstanding thst was almost inevitable when such completely different cultures were forced to live alongside each other. It resulted in a civil war, after which the Cumans moved on southwards, raiding and pillaging the Hungarians as they went (and thus seeming to justify the prejudice against them). This racially motivated conflict played into the hands of Batu and Subedei; the land into which they were marching was in a state of chaos before they had fired a single arrow.

Thus, in April 1241, three alien forces were converging on the Christian West. Within the space of forty-eight hours two great battles were fought which had shattering consequences for Europe. In the North the feudal leaders of an area now covering parts of Poland, Germany, Slovakia and the Czech Republic were gathering their forces to face the Mongol threat. The plan was to merge two armies led by Duke Henry II of Lower Silesia (known as 'Henry the Pious' or 'Henry the Bearded') and his brother-in-law, King Wenceslas I of Bohemia. As well as having their own soldiers under their command, they were joined by contingents of the Teutonic Knights and the Knights Templar. These were military orders of fighting monks, whose origins had been in the crusades to the Holy Land, men whose whole lives were dedicated to the defence of Christendom from incursion by Muslims, pagans and any other peoples who were enemies of the cross they wore on their tunics; men committed to the highest standards of discipline and professional prowess. These were

God's household cavalry. In addition Duke Henry had a contingent of gold miners (of whom more later). His total force numbered some 30,000 and Wenceslas would provided a further 50,000. That, they felt sure, should have been more than enough to see off 20,000 pagan nomads, for all the reputation they had gained. Probably it would have been, had the two European armies managed to combine.

Henry's fatal mistake was giving way to impatience, or perhaps nervousness. He was waiting at Liegnitz (modern Legnica), some seventy kilometres west of Breslau, for his brother-in-law to arrive. Had he had the benefit of a courier service comparable to Subedei's, he would have known exactly where Wenceslas was. Apparently he did not. So, instead of waiting in the safety of Liegnitz, he led his army south towards Jawor, in the hope of meeting the Bohemians on the road. Subedei knew exactly where Henry's reinforcements were – less than two days' march away. He, therefore, ordered an extra turn of speed from his host and intercepted Henry's army in an open plain called the Wahlstadt, on 9 April.

Henry disposed his forces as he would have done for any conventional European battle. They were drawn up in four squadrons of armoured cavalry with the gold miners attached to the front squadron. They were the expendable 'poor bloody infantry', who might absorb something of the first shock of an enemy charge. According to the 'rules' the Mongols should have launched a frontal attack with blood-curdling screams and the blare of trumpets and settled to hacking and thrusting at close quarters. Unfortunately, the Asiatic warriors had not read the rule book, or, rather, they had written their own. They galloped forward in small groups which were highly manoeuvrable, the only sound to be heard being the jingle of harness and the pounding of hooves. Because their army was split into numerous units, there was no target for the European knights to focus on, nothing against which to launch their ponderous charge. The enemy seemed to be a disorganised rabble of horsemen who dashed forward, fired their arrows from the saddle, then wheeled away. In fact, they were far from disorganised; they used pennants to signal to each other across the battlefield and were able to change tactics rapidly.

The first of Henry's squadrons, badly mauled by the barrage of arrows, pulled back and Henry sent in the second and third squadrons. They were much more successful – or so it seemed. But again they were outwitted by their enemy's tactics, which were designed to confuse the European horsemen. At first the Mongols retreated in apparent disorder, drawing Henry's cavalry after them in headlong pursuit. The dust created by thousands of hooves made visibility difficult. So when, out of the dust cloud, a rider came galloping towards them, shouting in Polish:

'Retreat! Retreat!' they did not recognise this as a trick to frighten the Polish-speaking knights. They turned back while their comrades wondered what was happening.

Duke Henry still had his fourth squadron, his reserves. These he now led forward in person, in order to restore some sense of order to the European ranks. This time he managed to come to grips with the enemy and hold them to man-to-man combat. His scattered horsemen recovered and joined in the fray, their superior numbers, at last, beginning to tell. Before long they had put the Mongols to rout, or – once again – so it seemed. Henry charged in pursuit across the plain. But the 'retreating' enemy now wheeled to right and left and began to pour deadly arrows on the European flanks. Not only that; they burned bundles of brushwood which sent clouds of smoke across the battlefield. The advancing knights had left their foot soldiers behind and now the two parts of Henry's army were invisible to each other. The only element in the knights' favour was their heavy armour, which was in some measure impervious to arrows. But the Mongols had an answer for that. They simply shot the horses, then hacked at the unwieldy knights as they struggled to fight on foot. Having disposed of the horsemen, it was a simple matter to turn their deadly attention to the unprotected infantry.

The carnage at Wahlstadt was terrible. Duke Henry was slain as he tried to flee from the battle and his severed head was paraded through the streets of Liegnitz on a lance, as a trophy. With him fell 25,000 men, the greater part of his entire army. The professional Knights Templar put up the stiffest resistance and were cut down to the last man.

And the Battle of Liegnitz was only a sideshow to the main confrontation. While Henry and his motley army were being slaughtered, King Béla was preparing for a showdown with the main Mongol army. He was not in the strongest of positions to face a new external threat because his own nation was in a state of political turmoil. In 1235 Béla IV had inherited from his father, Andrew II, a divided country. The nobility had forced Andrew to make considerable political concessions to his leading subjects and to make large grants of Crown land to them. Béla was determined to restore the power and dignity of the monarchy. He dismissed all his father's advisers and reversed several of his laws. To drive home his authority, he had all chairs removed from the council chamber so that dignitaries and petitioners were forced to stand in his presence. What made the king even less popular was his alliance with the Cumans. Béla used these nomads as a private army and this was one of the reasons for the frequent clashes between them and the Hungarian nobles.

When Béla attempted to gather his forces in Pest, his capital, to see off the coming invasion, he had only limited success. The Cumans had gone and several Hungarian nobles refused to raise troops for the king's army. Some actually wanted to see him defeated and killed. Duke Frederick of Austria and Styria offered his support – for a price – but proved to be unreliable and took his men home before the real fighting began. An advance guard of Mongols reached the suburbs of Pest in March and pillaged the area but Béla's forces were not yet ready to engage them. It was not until the end of the month that he was able to set out north-eastwards in search of the main Mongol army. The enemy retreated and seemed content to carry out skirmishing raids on the ponderously advancing European knights and infantry. What Béla did not know was that what he was chasing was only part of the Mongol horde. Batu and Subedei were waiting with most of their army in wooded land beyond the River Sajó, near the town of Mohi.

On 10 April 1241 Béla set up camp near the river, drawing his wagons into a circular stockade. A detachment of Hungarian cavalry advanced to the only river bridge and gave the defending Mongols a serious mauling as they tried to cross. However, as dawn broke on the 11th, the main Mongol army emerged from the wood on the opposite bank, equipped with stone-throwing catapults. They regained the bridge and streamed across. The Hungarians were caught almost completely unawares and hurriedly formed up to defend their position. Hours of hard fighting followed and the battle might have gone either way. However, Subedei had taken a force southwards along the river to seek another crossing point. Working through the night, his men constructed a bridge and crossed it to appear on the Hungarians' flank as the battle was at its hottest. Béla called his army back into the safety of the stockade. This was soon surrounded by the enemy.

The Hungarians found themselves hemmed in and subjected to a terrifying bombardment. The Mongols fired boulders, flaming arrows and incendiaries whose main ingredient was naphtha (a trick probably learned from the Chinese). This created panic throughout the camp. There was no way for the army to move out and form up to face the foe and Béla's men could only think of escape. Someone noticed that there was a gap in the Mongols' ring and men scrambled to get through it. But Batu had not left this opening by accident; he wanted to draw the enemy into the open so that his mobile horsemen could cut them down mercilessly as they fled. Béla's army was totally destroyed. Thousands upon thousands were killed. The numbers of combatants and casualties given in the records vary widely and there is no means now of assessing the figures involved. It seems likely that the two armies were fairly evenly matched numerically. Mongol losses were heavy but Hungarian fatalities were on a far worse scale. Hungary as a military power simply ceased to exist. More than that, the kingdom of Hungary ceased to exist. Béla IV escaped and did not stop running until he reached the Adriatic coast of Dalmatia, where he took refuge on an offshore island. The Mongol forces reconverged and made their leisurely and devastating way through the country. Some Hungarians shut themselves up in well-fortified cities and castles which the invaders did not bother to attack. But elsewhere they treated the inhabitants with utter ruthlessness. Where people offered resistance they were slaughtered. In one Dominican priory, where thousands of civilians had taken refuge, they slaughtered every man, woman and child, then piled their bodies on one bank of the Danube as an intimation to those beyond the river who might be considering evading capture. Those whom the Mongols did not kill they took as slaves. Between twenty and forty per cent of the Hungarian population perished either at the hands of their enemies or from the famine that Mongol rapine created.

Having stamped their authority on Hungary, Poland and Russia during the summer and autumn of 1241, and established a basic administrative system, Batu and Subedei swept onwards during the following winter. In determined pursuit of Béla they crossed the Danube, overran Croatia and only stopped when they reached the Adriatic. The borders of greater Mongolia were now a mere day's march from Vienna. Some of Subedei's scouts were actually captured in woodland close to the city. There was now little more than a thousand kilometres between the invaders and Rome or Paris or the new Brandenburg capital of Berlin. Considering the distances the Mongols had already covered, such centres of Christian civilisation were well within target range. There was no army that could have resisted them and these Christian civilisations were so absorbed in their own feuds and rivalries that they could not grasp the magnitude of the threat now facing them. When Béla IV appealed to his erstwhile ally, Frederick of Austria, the duke took him captive and demanded a large ransom for his release.

In fact, the western lands had no cause to worry. In the spring of 1242 the Great Khan, Ogodei, died in Karakorum. The great men of the empire had to gather to choose his successor – and to compete with each other for the crown. Batu ordered his men home, having first slaughtered thousands of prisoners. It may have been this that saved western Europe from the fate of eastern Europe. Or, possibly, Batu had no interest in pushing his boundaries still farther. He had discovered that one feature of life among these 'soft', settled, town-dwelling Christians would make it difficult to turn swift conquest into long-term occupation: his nomadic warriors were not equipped to deal with castles and fortified towns and cities. They were not experts in siege warfare. Hungary, Poland and the lands of their western neighbours were studded with such strongholds. They would always be centres of resistance. In fact, minor victories had been inflicted on the invaders by bands of Hungarian knights sallying forth from their fortresses. Cultural difference had enabled the Mongols to surprise and overwhelm their enemies, but there were clearly elements of western life that were more resistant.

For whatever reason, the lands over which Batu's horde had poured like an acid flood were saved further devastation. But what they had suffered came close to total obliteration. Thousands upon thousands of square kilometres of territory were depopulated and in ruins. Forest and semi-desert reclaimed land that had once been rich with cultivated crops. For several generations during the thirteenth and fourteenth centuries, these deserted settlements would have looked something like those images of ghost towns in the American "Wild West" that kept appearing on TV in the 1960s.

Béla IV spent the rest of his reign organising the partial recovery of Hungary. He learned some of the lessons of 1241–2. He re-established the Cumans. He applied the latest ideas about defensive architecture in building new castles and strengthening old ones. In 1261 he even defeated a Mongol raiding party. But when he died in 1270 the reconstruction of Hungary was still a work in progress.

The reason why an army of Europe's most experienced mounted troops was overwhelmed by a smaller force of Asiatic tribesmen was that they had not studied the battle tactics of their adversaries. 'Know your enemy' is a basic axiom of good generalship, but those who led Christendom's armies against the marauding 'devils' in 1241–2 completely underestimated the Mongols' military prowess, their tactical skill, their battlefield organisation and their courage. Much of this can be put down to the rudimentary means of communication available to them. Life within the cultural enclaves of what, in European chronology, we call the Middle Ages was self-contained in a way we can scarcely conceive now. Most people never travelled outside their own villages, let alone their own countries. In the popular imagination the world beyond the mountains, forests and oceans that fringed their own familiar reality was peopled by monsters, demons and freaks as weird and frightening as the aliens with which today's sci-fi film-makers populate distant galaxies. The Mongols, like the Chinese or the black tribesmen who lived beyond the African desert, were different, separate and obviously inferior. Why would one want to cultivate their acquaintance? They were not objects for colonisation. There were no commercial advantages to be gained by setting up trading connections with them. Even Christian missionaries, ever eager to spread their faith, were not falling over backwards to introduce the Prince of Peace to these warlike unbelievers.

But Europe's leaders cannot be completely exonerated for their ignorance of the newcomers pouring across their eastern borders. No diplomatic overtures were made towards them until 1245, when Pope Innocent IV sent envoys to Ogodei's successor. The messages that came back were crystal clear:

> From the rising of the sun to its setting, all the lands have been made subject to the Great Khan. You must say with a sincere heart, 'We will be your subjects; we will give you our strength.' You must come with your kings all together, without exception, to render us service and pay us homage... And if you do not follow the order of God and go against our orders, we will know you as our enemy.

Béla IV, who knew better than anyone what the Mongols were really like, sent warning messages to other rulers. They fell on deaf ears. One German prince who did take the situation seriously called upon his peers to unite in repentance and urgent, concerted action: 'Hear O islands and all the people of Christianity who profess our Lord's Cross, howl in ashes and sackcloth, in fasting, tears and mourning'. No one took any notice. To the modern reader it seems inconceivable that popes, emperors and princelings could fail to be spurred into concerted action by the horrors that had befallen their neighbours in 1241–2. But we should, perhaps, remind ourselves that even in the 1930s – a devastating world war still alive in the memory – the leaders of the democratic West persuaded themselves that totalitarian fascism and communism posed no real threat to their way of life.

Batu's armies certainly had their limitations. They were ill-equipped for mounting and sustaining sieges. They were far from home and their lines of supply and communication were extended. Such weaknesses could have been exploited by united and intelligent military leadership. Instead of this, the Mongols were, all too often, allowed to dictate the terms on which they fought. In open battle they could, literally, run rings round their opponents. This was not only because their ponies were small and fast and their armour light; their command structure was based on units of ten or so warriors working individually or in consort with other groups. The Mongols were not hidebound by old tried and tested tactics. Subedei displayed the imagination and flair that had given the Mongols victory over numerous foes – qualities manifestly lacking in the European generals who faced them in 1241–2. Perhaps the fundamental secret of Mongol success was that promotion depended on merit. In the tough school of nomadic warfare, a young warrior had to prove himself. There was no old-boy network providing easy access to the upper echelons of the military.

In thirteenth-century European society there were two classes: the military élite and everybody else. In peacetime the knight was a landowner who had an army of feudal dependents maintaining his household, tilling his fields and serving him in various other ways in exchange for his protection and permission to dwell on his land. When he went to war it was as the member of a military brotherhood united by the rules and conventions of chivalry. He rode a fine charger, carried a shield emblazoned with his coat of arms, was cocooned in thirty or forty kilograms of mail or plate armour, wore a helm that might be topped with a plume or heraldic device and was equipped with fearsome weapons – lance, broadsword and mace. It was all very splendid and the charge of a body of knights was certainly impressive. But there was no guarantee that the man inside the armour was as awe-inspiring as his outward show proclaimed. Admission to the ranks of the knightly class was on the basis of land-holding, not military skill.

When the knight went to war to fight for his prince, he conscripted men from his own estates to accompany him and make up the infantry. These 'soldiers' had no training, no uniform, no armour and no specialist weapons. The mounted knight, both physically and metaphorically, looked down on

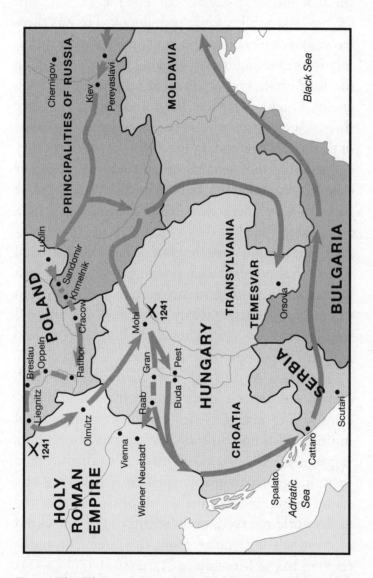

From The Times Atlas of World History, 1978, p.128

the foot soldier, meagrely equipped as he was with leather jerkin, pike, knife or billhook. He was there basically as a servant of the *real* army, a worker necessary for grooming horses, digging trenches, foraging for food and, in the thick of battle, despatching enemy knights who had been unhorsed by a lance thrust. Acts of heroism and bravery were not expected of this underclass and, in the awful, bewildering fury of battle the foot soldiers often lived down to their expectations, like the miners at Liegnitz. In their haste to save themselves from thundering hooves and flashing blades, they could clog up the battlefield. But so rigid were the class divisions in medieval society that no one thought it might be a good idea to train the infantry and incorporate them fully into the tactics of warfare. Only in the next century did the foot soldier wielding his deadly longbow begin to make an impact on military science.

The crisis of 1241–2 was, therefore, the clash of two cultures. A disciplined, ably led and efficient killing machine met a motley assortment of militias, with no common loyalty and bound by a vague, semi-Christian knightly code which served them ill against an enemy apparently devoid of any moral sense. In Latin the word for that part of the underworld reserved for the spirits of the worst kind of criminals is *tartarus*. From this time Europeans referred to the Mongols as 'Tartars'.

Chapter 3

1572

We are, unfortunately, familiar with what can happen when religious conviction becomes the motivating force for deeds of terrorism and other inhuman acts directed against people of different faiths or even different versions of the same faith. Few parts of the world have escaped persecution based on religious ideology. Particularly hideous is the marriage of religious conviction and state power. That is a frightening, oppressive and unholy thing. It is difficult to know which is worse, the use of threats, torture, informers, imprisonment and execution to compel belief or the insistence that such activity is not only condoned by, but actually ordered by 'God'.

In fact, state-sponsored religious persecution has very little to do with spiritual concerns and very much to do with the cohesion and preservation of political authority in this world. Niccolò Machiavelli, the sixteenth-century Italian philosopher, labelled religion 'the most necessary and assured support of any society' and, in most human cultures, it was a basic assumption that a tribe, nation or empire could thrive only with the support of its gods, and that the people must be diligent in their worship of those gods. The devastation wreaked by the power of religious fervour backed by military might has never been more apparent than in the activities of the regimes acting in the name of the Catholic Church in 1572. This year might be dubbed the 'year of reckonings'. Decades of control by state regimes backed and justified by the religious hierarchy of pope, bishops and priests faced serious challenges in several areas. We'll consider three of them, two in Europe and one in South America.

First, let us think about France. At the time it was politically vulnerable because it was under the rule of the unstable Valois dynasty – unstable for two reasons: dynastic weakness and religious division. Between 1547 and 1610 five kings reigned in succession – and died in lamentable circumstances. Henry II was killed in a jousting accident (1559) and was succeeded, in turn, by three of his sons. Francis II died of a brain tumour; Charles IX fell victim to tuberculosis; and Henry III was assassinated, as was his distant cousin who succeeded him as Henry IV. Throughout much of this period effective power was wielded by Henry II's widow, Catherine de Medici, but she was constantly hampered by noble factions at court – principally by the powerful Guise family, headed by the duc de Guise and his brother Jean, the cardinal de Lorraine.

The religious problem was created by the increasingly violent confrontations between French Protestants and the followers of traditional Catholicism. In the middle years of the sixteenth century, the Reformation had swept through Europe. It was a popular, grass-roots movement that challenged the religious assumptions on which papal power depended. The new Protestantism took various forms but the brand which was most influential in Switzerland, France, the Netherlands, England and Scotland was Calvinism (after the French theologian, John Calvin). In France, especially in the southern half of the country, Calvinism spread with amazing rapidity. The new-style Christianity could claim two million adherents (commonly known as Huguenots) by 1572 and in at least two thousand churches they practised their simpler form of worship.

One of the characteristics of Calvinism was an abhorrence of ornate ritual and, particularly, of painted and sculpted images of God, Jesus, the Virgin Mary and the saints. From time to time the more headstrong devotees of this 'purer'-style religion carried out iconoclastic (i.e. image-breaking) attacks on Catholic churches in order to smash the objects of 'idolatry' – stained-glass windows, highly coloured statues and altars decked with gold and silver ornaments. Traditionalist communities were not slow to react. Egged on by their priests, zealous Catholics took bloody reprisals against their hated Huguenot neighbours. By the 1560s there was open feuding between rival groups on the streets of many towns and cities. Hate-filled sermons thundered from rival pulpits and inflammatory pamphlets were widely distributed. But this was not a case of 'six of one and half a dozen of the other'; Protestants vented their spleen almost entirely on things. Catholic individuals and mobs deliberately butchered people. Instructed by their spiritual leaders – including the pope himself – Catholics believed they were purging the nation of a dangerous disease, a spiritual plague that had to be eradicated to prevent it becoming an unstoppable epidemic. Any means were justified by these ends – including murder. Hundreds of Huguenots were killed in mini-massacres throughout France. But worse was to come. What made it difficult for the authorities to deal with these disorders was that many noble families and civic leaders had taken sides. It was not just working people and minor tradesmen who had adopted the Huguenot faith; the whole of French society from top to bottom was split by the religious conflict. Several major towns and cities were ruled by Huguenot oligarchies, and Calvinists as well as traditionalists had their defenders among leading courtiers and ministers. The Guise family headed up the Catholic faction in France and the Huguenots were led by the duc de Condé and Admiral Gaspard de Coligny.

The king and the queen regent, Catherine de Medici, who desperately wanted to keep order, were caught in the middle and struggling to keep control of rival factions. In 1572 Charles IX, who had been king for twelve years, was a sickly young man under his mother's control. She was determined that France's powerful, feuding noble families should be kept loyal to the Crown but that was not easy when she had already buried two kings and when many believed that Charles was not long for this world. The country was in a state of virtual civil war and the royal council was hopelessly divided. Catherine judged that her only chance of survival lay in bringing the two sides together, patching up a peace and hoping that it would last. Her efforts could not possibly have had a more disastrous outcome.

Catherine arranged a marriage between her ten-year-old daughter, Marguerite, and the eighteen-year-old Henry of Navarre, who would be next in line to the throne in the event of Catherine's remaining sons dying childless. Henry was the acknowledged leader of France's Huguenots and Catherine thought that if she could keep him at her court his followers in the Pyrenean province of Navarre would not be able to make trouble. On the face of it this was a shrewd political move, an attempt to base judgement on pragmatism rather than religious emotion. But, even while guests were gathering for the celebrations, news was brought to Catherine that may well have caused her to ponder her chances of success. A woman styling herself a prophetess was reported to be drawing crowds to her ecstatic preaching. Her message was very simple: she had, she said, been charged with warning Parisians of God's wrath if any concession was made to heretics. Unless every last Huguenot was exterminated, she proclaimed, Paris would go up in all-consuming flames. The queen regent took the risk. The wedding was held in mid-August before all the leading nobles of the realm. These included most of the nation's prominent Huguenots. But the queen mother had either miscalculated or she had become part of a plot to deal decisively with the Huguenot 'menace'. At the very least, bringing together the Montagues and Capulets of French society could only create a highly charged atmosphere in the capital. News had already reached Paris of bloody confrontations in the Netherlands and this had turned the screw of public anger and anxiety. A Catholic gunman shot and wounded Coligny in a Paris street. Now the Guises and their supporters feared a Protestant backlash. As the admiral took to his bed, the rumour rapidly spread that he and his friends were planning savage reprisals, including the capture or assassination of the king and his replacement by Navarre. The Guises actually encouraged the rumour and used it to persuade Charles and his mother that they would have to make a pre-emptive strike.

On the night of 23–24 August guards sealed off land exits from Paris and chains were stretched across the Seine to prevent unauthorised departure by river. Next morning, St Bartholomew's Day, royal troops, led by the duc de Guise, broke into Coligny's lodging. The admiral was hacked to death in his bedroom, his body mutilated and thrown out into the courtyard. Members of the household who had not managed to escape across the roof were similarly treated. Guise then led his men to other quarters of the city where members of Coligny's entourage were lodged. How far the Catholic leadership intended to go is not known but the sight of mounted troops shouting triumphantly and waving bloody trophies was all that was needed to unleash ordinary Parisians in an orgy of murder, rape, torture and robbery. Shouting, 'Kill! Kill!' and brandishing religious pictures and emblems, they broke into the houses of known Huguenots, dragged them into the street and demonstrated just what the human animal is capable of when its baser emotions are aroused.

Francis Walsingham, English ambassador to the royal court, was awakened by the sound of terrified men and women hammering on his door and begging for asylum. From them he heard and reported home several tales of gut-wrenching atrocities. One typical story told how a Protestant merchant, Mathurin Lussault, was stabbed on his own doorstep. His son was hacked to pieces. His wife leaped from an upstairs window to escape the assassins, broke her legs and was dragged from the courtyard by her hair. Her hands were cut off so that her captors could appropriate her bangles. She was then impaled on a spit and paraded through the streets before being thrown into the river, already streaked red with Huguenot blood. As the mayhem spread outwards from its epicentre, such incidents were repeated over and over again, while church bells rang out in exultant triumph. Catholic bloodlust was not sated for three days, by which time some two thousand Parisians had been massacred. But the horror was far from over. As news of the events of St Bartholomew's Day reached other towns and cities, the gruesome incidents were replicated by provincial vigilantes. More than five thousand men, women and children perished for having the temerity to believe a form of Christianity at variance with traditional Catholicism. Back in the capital, Henry of Navarre, the bridegroom whose nuptials had led to the holocaust, was forced, on pain of death, to convert. What happened in France during the Terror (the worst period of the French Revolution) is well known and the subject of numerous books (for example, Dickens' *Tale of Two Cities*), films and plays but the St Bartholomew's Day Massacre which preceded it by 221 years was, in some ways, worse, and the total death count was not very different.

But fervour and bloodlust were not limited to France as they were during the turbulance of 1793; they constituted a Europe-wide experience.

> Before suffering the slightest damage to religion and the service of God, I would lose all my estates, and a hundred lives if I had them, because I do not propose, nor do I desire to be the ruler of heretics. If it can be, I will try to settle the matter of religion without taking up arms, because I fear that to do so would lead to their total ruin. But if I cannot settle matters as I wish, without force, I am determined to go in person and take charge of everything, and neither the danger nor the destruction of those provinces, nor of all the rest I possess, can deter me from this end.

Chilling words from a chilling man. Philip II of Spain presided, in the name of God, over an empire incorporating a large part of Europe and conquered territories in the Americas. Austere and

devout, His Most Catholic Majesty (a hereditary
title granted by the pope, which he took very seriously) had a rigid, self-denying devotion to duty
which bordered on paranoia. Like some Christian
ayatollah, he saw himself as chosen for the sacred
mission of extending and purifying the traditional faith of western Europe and, in his letter
to the pope, quoted above, he promised to clear
the Spanish Netherlands (modern Holland and
Belgium) of pestilential Protestants. Eradicating
heresy was a vital aspect of his vocation. His was
an exalted and lonely mission, demanding great
self-sacrifice. It was symbolised by the severely
functional headquarters he had built for himself
in a sparsely populated part of the Spanish sierra,
north of Madrid. The Escorial was both a palace
and a monastery. It was not designed with extravagant court entertainments in mind, such as were
indulged in by contemporary monarchs. Philip
observed a strict regime of long hours at his desk
interspersed with religious devotions. A squint
(an internal window) in his bedchamber enabled
him to look directly down on the high altar of
the monastery so that he would never be far
away from the worshipping heart of the Escorial
complex. The writer and poet, G.K. Chesterton
later depicted the king as a sinister, manipulating
being despatching his instructions via subservient
minions from his tomb-like residence:

The walls are hung with velvet that is black and
    soft as sin,
And little dwarfs creep out of it and little dwarfs
    creep in.
He holds a crystal phial that has colours like the
    moon,
He touches and it tingles, and he trembles very
    soon,
And his face is as a fungus of a leprous white and
    grey
Like plants in the high houses that are sheltered
    from the day,
And death is in the phial…

Philip, certainly, dealt in death from his remote
retreat – death of individuals and whole communities. It was a responsibility he had inherited from
his father, Charles V, during whose reign over two
thousand Protestants had been killed in the Low
Countries (the Netherlands), the most trouble-
some corner of his empire. Yet Charles had failed
to eradicate heresy. By the time Philip inherited the
major part of his father's empire in 1558, Calvinism
had made considerable strides in the Spanish
Netherlands.

This northern part of his dominions was very
important both economically and politically. It was
a major commercial nation; its prosperous burgers
maintained long-distance land and sea trade routes

with the Levant, from which came exotic spices, gemstones and oriental silks, while their contacts with the Baltic supplied them with timber, flax and pitch (all vital for the building of ocean-going ships). And Philip's wealthy Dutch subjects were, of course, a vital source of the taxation he needed to pay the mounting costs of his empire. Politically the region was important because it enabled Spain to keep a check on its traditional rival for European domination – France. Spain and the Netherlands were like the upper and lower jaws of a geographical vice. Applying pressure could restrain French ambitions. Philip, therefore, had no intention of relinquishing his hold on the Netherlands.

The Netherlanders, of course, had a different perspective. They resented their occupation by a foreign power, an occupation which had often been sustained by cruel acts of suppression. Over the years there had been sporadic revolts and the spread of Calvinism had been one expression of fervent nationalism. Just as for Catherine and Charles, the existence of Protestantism was something that threatened to break up the nation into regional units, so for Philip it appeared to be an arrogant, defiant force that might tear a gaping hole in his patrimony. And then there was the international dimension to the problem. As Europe divided ever more rigidly into Catholic and Protestant camps, religious minorities were succoured by their co-religionists abroad. Preachers arrived in the Netherlands from Switzerland. Huguenots fleeing persecution in France crossed the border into Philip's territory, and sporadic purges sent refugees seeking asylum in England. At the Escorial the self-appointed champion of Rome fumed at the encouragement his heretical subjects received from other lands. He had already begun to ponder a long-term plan to 'deal' with England and this would take final shape in the Grand Armada of 1588.

For the moment, however, he had enough on his plate bringing his own subjects to heel. That was difficult for several reasons. Any military presence, to be effective, had to be planned on a large scale: the terrain of the Low Countries posed enormous problems for any commander. One traveller described it as 'the great bog of Europe… a universal quagmire… the buttocks of the world, full of veins and blood, but no bones'. The Low Countries were, as the name suggests, lands of below-sea-level meadows, marsh, rivers and dykes. Population was centred in well-fortified towns and cities. Moving armies over such country and sustaining them during long sieges was an arduous business. And expensive. And that was Philip's other problem: he was broke. Gold and silver arrived every year in the fleets from the Americas, which unloaded their glittering cargoes on the quayside at Cadiz, much of it destined for the royal treasury, but the costs of sustaining the administration of Spain's widespread dominions swallowed up all the government's resources and more. The truth was that Philip was financially and politically overstretched. As well as his possessions in Spain, northern Europe and the New World, he ruled a large part of Italy and several Mediterranean islands. In this latter area he was being challenged by the westward spread of the Turkish Ottoman Empire. 'The Turk' was the big bogeyman of Europe. Ever since the Muslims had captured Constantinople, ancient capital of the eastern Christian empire, in 1453, they had set their sights on overrunning the rest of the continent, sporadically advancing by sea and land. Philip regarded it as part of his duty to stop the advance of this heathen empire and he was constantly having to divert money and troops to the Mediterranean theatre of war. His need for cash forced him to confront another difficulty in the Netherlands – the States General. This was the regional parliament that had to endorse and levy any taxes the king called for. Inevitably, the members of this body resented demands for money which would be used to strengthen Spain's hold on their country.

George Santayana, the twentieth-century philosopher, defined a fanatic as someone who redoubles his effort when he has lost sight of his objective. Philip II had not so much lost sight of his objective as taken on a responsibility far in excess of his abilities and his resources. Atlas-like, he shouldered the burden of Catholic Christendom, and if he unrealistically redoubled his efforts it was because, shut up in his elaborate hermitage, he was so obsessed with his 'divine mission' that he could not properly evaluate it. The tragedy was that his miscalculation cost thousands of lives.

Because he was temperamentally incapable of religious toleration but lacked the resources to force strict Catholicism on all his subjects, Philip did the worst thing he could have done: he threatened what he could not perform. He announced that heresy would be vigorously resisted and that the Inquisition would be given more manpower. This could only arouse resentment and encourage reaction. Protestants believed that their faith was under threat but that the threat was a weak one. From the mid-1560s Calvinist preachers became more bold and conversions more frequent. Outbreaks of iconoclasm followed; groups of zealots entered Catholic churches and removed statues, paintings, altar cloths and other evidence of 'superstition'. Philip's regent in the Netherlands, the Duchess of Parma, wrote panic-stricken, exaggerated letters, telling him that half the country was in revolt. The pope urged him to go in person to his troubled province and restore order 'before it is too late'. The regent may have been overstating the case but her analysis of the political situation was faultless: either the king must grant religious toleration or he must restore true religion by force.

Philip was in a state of confusion but, at last, he had a stroke of luck. Pressure on the empire's eastern frontier relaxed when the Turkish sultan died and the Ottoman Empire was riven by revolts and mutinies. Now, at last, Philip could spare troops to be sent to the Netherlands. He gathered a large army but instead of leading it himself, he appointed someone who was the wrong man for the job. Don Fernando Álvarez de Toledo, Duke of Alva, was a haughty, sixty-year-old Spanish grandee, with a vivid streak of cruelty, who had a pathological hatred of heresy and a xenophobic contempt for all things not Spanish. He arrived in 1567 and set about instituting a reign of terror. When the Duchess of Parma protested at his excesses, Philip backed the duke, whereupon the duchess resigned and took herself into comfortable retirement in Italy. There were now no moderating influences to soften Alva's cruelty. He arrested almost 9,000 people and had them tried by special tribunals. More than a thousand were executed for heresy or treason. But he failed to lay hands on the actual or potential leaders of nationalist revolt. The wealthier Netherlanders and also those who valued their religion above the comforts of home life fled for asylum to other Protestant lands. As many as 100,000 departed during the 1560s. This included several members of the nobility and their acknowledged commander, William the Silent, Prince of Orange. At his refuge in Germany he gathered around him a court in exile, obtained money from foreign sympathisers and assembled a force of patriots ready to fight for their country's independence. For the moment there was little he could do but carry out lightning raids on Spanish garrisons but the prince became the focus of all those who hoped to see a free Netherlands – and of those who hoped to see a Calvinist Netherlands. They began to sing a new song – the Wilhelmus. It took the form of an address from William to his people:

> Let no despair betray you,
> My subjects true and good.
> The Lord will surely stay you
> Though now you are pursued.
> He who would live devoutly
> Must pray God day and night
> To throw his power about me
> As champion of your right.

So ran one of the song's many verses. Years later the Wilhelmus would become the Dutch national anthem.

The situation in the Netherlands in the late 1560s was reminiscent of that of France under the Nazi heel in the early 1940s. An underground resistance distributed anti-Spanish propaganda and carried out acts of sabotage against the regime. Alva responded by imposing swingeing taxes, stationing garrisons throughout the country and making fearful examples of 'troublemakers'. His actions fuelled increasing resentment and mounting hope of deliverance. And, in 1572, the fight back began in earnest.

Just as the Nazis in 1944 held their occupied lands in a vice-like grip, were invincible by land but vulnerable to attack from the sea, so Alva, though seemingly in complete control, had his Achilles heel. A fleet of rebels calling themselves the Sea-Beggars patrolled the North Sea coast from bases in England and, on 1 April, they struck. The first target was the town of Brill. How would they be received? The citizenry certainly feared reprisals. If they opened their gates to the rebels and the rising failed they were in no doubt about the vengeance Alva would exact. Yet so great was their hatred of Catholic Spain that patriotic feelings outweighed concern for their own safety. The majority welcomed their deliverers and joined in venting their fury on representatives of the alien regime. They looted churches and slaughtered nineteen Catholic priests. From this bridgehead the Sea-Beggars spread out by land and sea, the towns coming over to them more readily as their success accelerated. William the Silent sent troops and messages of support, and it is a measure of the strength of anti-Spanish feeling that by the autumn all of the northern Netherlands, except Rotterdam and Delft, was in rebel hands and had accepted William as its lawful ruler.

Everywhere the Sea-Beggars and their supporters took control there were reprisals against the agents of Philip and the pope, although William issued orders against lynch law and mob violence. Alva did not show the same restraint. He only understood one way to establish authority – instilling fear. By September he was able to set about the work of reconquest. The nationalists' problem was that they lacked the men and materiel to hold all their towns and cities against determined siege. The first rebel centre to fall into the general's hands was Mons, and he used its capture as an opportunity to show other towns what they could expect by continued resistance. He gave his men carte blanche to pillage, rape and murder at will. Anyone spared was forced to reconvert to Catholicism. Events followed the same course at Zutphen in November. On 2 December Alva regained Naarden and ordered the annihilation of every man, woman and child in the town. By the year's end the Netherlands was reduced to a state of social and political disintegration, economic collapse and untold misery. Months later King Philip removed Alva from his command, but it was too late to salve the bitterness that the last few years, and the last few months in particular, had driven deep into the soul of the nation. The war of independence was destined to rumble on for another thirty years but there would be no forgetting the events of 1572.

This was also the year that Spanish political ambition and religious fervour brought about the final overthrow of the Inca civilisation of Peru. The colonisation of the South American indigenous kingdoms had begun fifty years earlier and Hernando Pizarro, the Spanish conqueror, had made contact with the mighty Andean empire of the Incas in 1527. He discovered a well-organised and wealthy state, covering thousands of square kilometres of mountainous and forest terrain, incorporating some twelve million subjects from several tribes, and with an infrastructure of roads and administrative centres. This disparate empire was of quite recent origin. It was less than a hundred years since the Incas of the Cuzco valley had extended their rule over neighbouring peoples, but they governed with an impressive efficiency from their capital in the high Andes. The main element in the political cement holding the empire together was religion. The Incas worshipped a pantheon of spirits of which the most important was Punchao, the god of the rising sun. The Inca king was believed to be a son of the deity, the spiritual as well as the political focus of the nation. Worship was elaborate, consisting of intricate rituals carried out by a cult of priests and involving animal and (occasionally) human sacrifice. Within a few years this remarkable civilisation had been crushed by the first Spanish conquerors (the *conquistadores*). But the Europeans, being little more than a bunch of squabbling, greedy, power-hungry thugs, could not effectively rule the domains that they had grabbed in the name of the Spanish king. Controlled exploitation on behalf of the Crown was left to later generations of administrators sent out from Madrid.

By the 1560s stable and peaceful government of the province had been established. Most of the tribes had been pacified and, thanks to the labours of Catholic missionaries, most of them had been converted. That is to say, they had submitted to baptism and dutifully attended mass. How deep their submission was to the new religion is a matter of conjecture. The monks and friars who worked among the forest and mountain peoples built their churches on the sites of existing shrines, they adapted Inca decorative motifs and festivities and they used native music – all in order to ease the transition to the new religion. But hearts and minds had certainly not been completely won over. Just as tribesmen had meekly accepted the beliefs of the powerful Inca conquerors, so they now acknowledged the God of their more powerful European masters. The Spanish authorities were well aware that much of the old worship continued in secret at sacred places deep in the forest, but this did not matter as long as the natives were quiescent.

Of greater concern was the existence of a semi-independent Inca state. Cuzco had been taken over as the seat of the colonial administration but the old regime was still very much intact, though its power was considerably reduced. The reigning king, Titu Cusi, had his capital in the remote jungle city of Vilcabamba, some three or four hundred kilometres from Cuzco, and here he continued to preside over the ancient rituals. At the sacred shrine stood a full-sized golden image of the god, Punchao. Within it, according to one traveller, was

a golden chalice [containing] a powder made from the hearts of dead Incas [i.e. kings]… it is surrounded by a form of golden medallions in order that, when struck by the sun, these should shine in such a way that one could never see the idol itself, but only the reflected brilliance of these medallions.

Titu Cusi himself, when he magnanimously granted audience to Spanish representatives, was scarcely less resplendent. His head was circled with a golden diadem surmounted by a crest of many-coloured feathers. Silver and gold plaques adorned his chest and feathered ornaments were fastened to his legs. He carried a shield, spear and dagger, all of gold. As long as this impressive representative of the old ways continued to enjoy his independence, the King Philip's men could not feel a hundred per cent secure. There was always a chance that the Peruvian tribes would revert to Inca allegiance. The viceroy made repeated attempts to get Titu Cusi baptised and to declare his allegiance unequivocally to the Spanish king. Above all, they tried to lure him out of his remote headquarters so that they could control his activities. But the Inca leader was too smart for them. He received missionaries and official embassies. He discussed at great length the terms of a new treaty but he held on firmly to his independence – and he stayed put. He respected the power of the Europeans but he had no reason to trust them or to like them. His father had been imprisoned by the conquistadores until he paid a huge ransom and was subsequently murdered in his own home by visitors to whom he had offered his hospitality. His mother and sister had been systematically raped. Many of his own people had been slaughtered in wars and attacks on their villages.

But not all Spaniards who pioneered the spread of Christian culture to the New World were ruthless colonialists. Many missionaries found themselves on the side of the natives. Foremost among them was Bartolomé de Las Casas, a colonial bishop. Throughout a long life, most of which was spent in the Americas (he died in 1566, aged ninety-two), he was a thorn in the flesh of the Spanish administrators. He wrote frequent reports to Spain, denouncing the cruel and unchristian behaviour of the king's representatives, and in books such as his *Historia de las Indias* he pointed out that such inhumanity was not only immoral but was not the way to go about converting heathens to belief in the God of love. Las Casas and his friends had many supporters in Spain and not a few at the royal court. Successive viceroys were called to account by the king as a result of accusations made by the missionaries. This did not make for good relations with the local administrators in Peru, who felt that they were enduring the discomforts of life among alien people in a steamy, fever-ridden environment in order to enrich their own king, only to find themselves bad-mouthed by interfering do-gooders. In their perception the local peoples, particularly the Incas, were very far from being the innocent and put-upon prey of a distant hostile power. Francisco de Toledo, who arrived in Peru as viceroy in 1569, justified his hardline policy by pointing out that the Incas were not the legitimate rulers of the Peruvian people. They were comparative newcomers who had set up a harsh regime, were far crueller than their European successors and used religion as a tool to keep their subjects in slavery. There was a little truth in Toledo's protest – but only a little. To visitors from Spain, especially those returning to Peru after a few years' absence, the evidence of their own eyes forced them to a different conclusion:

> We cannot conceal the great paradox that a barbarian kept such excellent order that the entire country was calm and well nourished, whereas today we see only infinite deserted villages on all the roads of the kingdom.

Tens of thousands of men, women and children had perished in war or as a result of ill-treatment at the hands of the Spaniards or had been shipped off to slave labour in Caribbean plantations.

Toledo was determined to put an end, once and for all, to the Inca puppet kingdom, and events at Vilcabamba played into his hands. In 1571 Titu Cusi died unexpectedly. His people were devastated, though they should not really have been surprised; for years the king had abused his body with every kind of indulgence. This had two immediate results. In their grief, the Inca people looked around for scapegoats and the word soon spread that their king had been poisoned by a Spanish friar, Diego Ortiz. The poor man was grabbed and subjected to the most appalling tortures. First he was lashed to a cross and whipped. Then a hole was bored in his jaw and a rope passed through it. By this he was led on a long journey to be presented to the new king, Tupac Amaru. Somehow, Ortiz survived this ordeal. But when he arrived at his journey's end, naked, weak and mud-spattered, he had no chance to protest his innocence. Tupac Amaru ordered his execution. The friar was quickly despatched and buried head-down in a pit with a spear stuck into his rectum. The accession of a hostile, anti-Spanish king was the second result of Titu Cusi's death. Tupac Amaru was dedicated to the old religion and had a profound hatred of the conquerors. There was to be no further pretence of negotiation.

Toledo was unaware of the change of regime at Vilcabamba and, in March 1572, he sent a 'final' embassy to the Inca chief, demanding that he come to Cuzco for the signing of a lasting agreement with the Spanish Crown. His representative was Atilano de Anaya, a man well versed in liaison with the Incas. He was met at the Vilcabamba border by Inca officials who told him that the king would receive him as long as he came alone. Tupac Amaru was playing the same game as Toledo; making the enemy vulnerable. What followed is recorded in a report sent back to Spain:

> The Indians made him a hut on a small hill and brought him some food to eat. They told him on behalf of the Inca that he should wait there for three days... He spent the time sitting on an outcrop of rock beside his hut in such a way that he was seen by Diego, a Negro in his service whom the Indians had not allowed to cross with him... that night they killed him with their lances and threw him down a ravine... When day came [Diego] crossed the bridge

and went in the hut but did not find his master's bed or clothing. Following a path he saw Anaya dead and thrown into a small gulley... Fearing that they would do the same to him he crossed back over the bridge and took the road to Cuzco. [On the way he reported to the local mission priest, who] sent Indians [for the body] which they brought and he buried.

This atrocity gave Toledo the *cassus belli* he wanted. He sent a military expedition to Vilcabamba to expedite the final showdown. Theirs was a hellish ordeal. They clambered up mountains, slithered down into ravines, waded through treacherous swamps and hacked through dense jungle. Much of the time they were labouring at altitudes of more than 3,000 metres, which was particularly tough for European soldiers whose bodies were not adjusted to coping with the thin atmosphere. They were harassed on their march by attacks from Tupac Amaru's forces and had to face one pitched battle. But they pressed on and the natives retreated before them, unable to withstand the murderous fire of Spanish arquebuses. One by one the tribes were either conquered or won over. Eventually the campaign became a simple matter of pursuing the king, who was fleeing deeper into his territory, accompanied by his pregnant wife and a diminishing band of supporters. Trecking along jungle paths and canoeing down

fast-flowing rivers, often at night, the pursuers eventually caught up with the exhausted Tupac Amaru,
huddled over a camp fire.

It was at the end of September 1572 that the
last proud Inca king, son of the sun god, was
marched in chains through the city that had
been the capital of his ancestors. Also borne
along in the triumphal procession were the
mummified bodies of two previous kings, chests
of gold ornaments and the glowing statue of the
god Punchao. The humiliation of the Incas was
complete, the superiority of the Spaniards incon-
trovertibly demonstrated, the pre-eminence of
the Christian God proved beyond doubt. Was
that sufficient? Not for Francisco de Toledo. Two
things were wanting to drive home the finality
of the conquest. First of all, monks were sent to
Tupac Amaru's prison cell to convert him to the
Catholic faith. It did not prove a difficult task.
The last Inca readily accepted the religion of the
conquerors, doubtless hoping that, by receiving
baptism and becoming 'one of them', his captors
might be persuaded to treat him leniently. But the
second thing that Toledo was determined upon
was the Inca's death. He was convinced that the
colonial regime could never be secure as long as a
potential rival to Spanish rule existed. Even while
Tupac Amaru was receiving Christian instruc-
tion he was standing trial. Toledo understood

well that speed was of the essence. If the king was allowed to languish indefinitely in prison, popular sentiment might well swing round in his favour. Among the viceroy's own advisers there were those advocating the mercy that, they suggested, would become the representative of a Christian king. But Toledo was not to be moved. A hurried trial was arranged and the prisoner was charged with a whole raft of heinous offences, for the majority of which he could not remotely be considered responsible. At the end of the fiasco the judge dutifully pronounced the accused guilty and ordered the death sentence.

This was the signal for a wave of protest to come rolling into the viceroy's court. The whole city was shocked. No less than nine leading ecclesiastics went down on their knees before Toledo to beg for a remission of sentence. If the viceroy feared Tupac Amaru's influence, surely he could be sent back to Spain as proof that the Inca problem had been solved once and for all? Let King Philip determine his fate, they urged. It was all to no avail. Within days the prisoner was taken under armed escort to a scaffold erected in the city square and there, before an enormous crowd, many of whom must have re-alised that they were witnesses of a historic event, he was beheaded. According to a Spanish chronicler (who might well be suspected of wishing to gild the lily), Tupac made a final speech in which he denounced the traditional worship of his people as a sham.

This solemn event was but the apogee of a campaign designed to exterminate all vestiges of Inca religion. Hundreds of Tupac Amaru's relatives and principal officers were rounded up and executed. The remaining Inca shrines were razed. The mummified bodies of past kings were burned. And, of course, every example of gold ritual vessels that could be found was appropriated. The statue of Punchao was sent back to Spain as a gift for King Philip.

By the mid-sixteenth century the pope, the leader of Catholic Christendom, had long since exchanged the simple shoes of the fisherman for the hob-nailed boots of the soldier. In league with powerful monarchs like the rulers of Spain and France, successive Roman pontiffs had extended their authority over much of Europe and, indeed, they claimed universal dominion, so that the cross was planted wherever greed and opportunism took discoverers and conquistadores. But there was a price to be paid. They suffered the fate of the young lady of Riga,

> Who rode, with a smile, on a tiger.
> They returned from the ride
> With the lady inside
> And the smile on the face of the tiger.

The irenic gospel of the suffering Saviour had been gobbled up – or at least smothered – by the hatred, violence, arrogance and avarice that are the inevitable characteristics of terrestrial authorities and especially of expansionist regimes. The appalling events of 1572 forcefully illustrate what happens when men try to mix the oil and water of secular and religious power.

Chapter 4

1631–2

When we, the Workers, all demand:
'What are WE fighting for?'
Then, then we'll end that stupid crime,
That devil's madness – War

Robert Service

The question of why we go to war is one which today's leaders *do* feel the need to answer. However unconvincing their excuses (think, for example, of the controversy that surrounded Bush and Blair's reasons for waging war with Iraq in 2003), this is – in a perverse way – encouraging. They generally put on a good show of presenting the reasons for fighting (and, indeed, they may even end up convincing themselves). They have to; that is the benefit of democracy.

Our ancestors were not so fortunate. The major wars of past centuries were fought by power-obsessed autocrats who sent their armies against each other with no regard for their subjects, whose sons were conscripted, whose crops, sheep, cattle and poultry were commandeered, whose fields were trampled into mud, whose wives and daughters were abused by billeted soldiery, and who had to suffer the aftermath of disease and famine. Statesmen could talk of victory or defeat. For the ordinary people, war was always a catastrophe.

Because they loom large in the popular imagination, the two world wars of the twentieth century are often thought to have had a particularly devastating effect on population. But in terms of military and civilian fatalities, the Thirty Years War was far more destructive. Sixty million people died in the Second World War, which is a staggering and sobering number. But it represents only 3.5 per cent of the population of the nations involved. Fewer people died in the Thirty Years War: seven and a half million. But this figure represents 35 per cent of the population of the combatant nations.

This conflict lasted from 1618 to 1648 and involved all the leading European nations. It was, in fact, the nearest catastrophe to a world war that the European powers witnessed in the era before explorers offered up farther parts of the planet to colonisation. It was caused by clashing cultures or ambitions – territorial expansionism, religious rivalry, dynastic scheming. And its impact was truly appalling.

It destroyed thousands of villages and towns in what is now Germany. It shattered cities and condemned inhabitants to generations of rebuilding. It made ploughland unworkable. It dislocated commerce. It littered field and meadow, highway and urban street with corpses. And it condemned the physically and mentally shattered to the scrap-heap of the unemployable. I propose to put just one dismal year of the Thirty Years War under the microscope to demonstrate how bestial 'civilised' men can be when they are manipulated by leaders who have their own agendas.

Some background first. It all began with a bungled political protest in Bohemia (modern Czech Republic). On 23 May 1618 an angry mob stormed into Hradčany Castle, Prague's administrative centre, and climbed the staircase to the council chamber. They grabbed hold of the two imperial officials they had come to find and dragged them towards the casement window. 'Jesu Maria, help!' screamed Jaroslav Martinitz, as he was hoisted over the sill and flung into space. Moments later Vilem Slavata and his unfortunate secretary were following his terrifying descent. Then anticlimax. As the exultant rebels stared down into the court-yard they saw their victims stagger to their feet and make good their escape. They had landed in what some accounts refer to as a heap of horse manure but which may, in fact, not have had its origins in any four-legged animal. The lives, though not the dignity of the emperor's representatives, were thus saved.

Bohemia was a state within the empire that enjoyed a large measure of independence. The state religion was Protestant, but its crown had just passed to an ardent Catholic who believed God had spoken to him directly and ordered him to launch a crusade against 'heretical' Protestants. This was the Archduke Ferdinand of Styria, who became the Holy Roman Emperor, Ferdinand II, the next year. From Vienna the emperor ruled over a vast area from the Baltic to the Adriatic, from the North Sea to the River Oder, and comprising all or parts of modern Germany, Austria, Hungary, Serbia, Croatia, the Czech state, North Italy and Belgium. Reared by Jesuits, Ferdinand was described by the historian C. V. Wedgwood as 'one of the boldest and most single-minded politicians that the Habsburg dynasty ever produced'. The forty-year-old ruler was not a wild-eyed fanatic. Those who knew him well described him as an affable, charming man who displayed what we might now call a rather 'old-fashioned' courtesy, a prince who lived frugally and shunned display. It was the irresistible logic of his faith as taught by his priestly mentors that convinced him that he had a sacred destiny to fulfil and that that destiny involved ridding his realm of Protestants. He had sent Martinitz and Slavata to

Prague as his regents, with instructions to end the toleration hitherto extended to Protestants. When they were stormed by the mob, he could not ignore the insult. But he could not have known how far-reaching and calamitous the consequences of his reaction would be. The bizarre, bungled assassination attempt, known to history as the Defenestration (literally 'the throwing out of a window') of Prague, set in train a sequence of bloody events which were to convulse the continent for three decades.

Almost exactly a hundred years earlier, Martin Luther, a monk in the Saxon town of Wittenberg, had challenged the authority of the pope and begun the Reformation. That movement created in Europe, in rough and ready terms, a north-south divide. Scandinavia, England, Scotland, the Low Countries, several Swiss cantons and much of Germany, Poland, Bohemia and Hungary embraced Protestantism, while the rest of the continent remained loyal to the pope. From round about 1580, Europe was torn by sporadic wars of religion. The pope spurred on loyal Catholic rulers to expunge the 'curse of heresy'. Protestant kings and freedom fighters, determined to retain their independence from Rome, fought back in the name of 'conscience'. Inevitably, this meant religion getting tangled up with nationalism, because state rulers decided which version of Christianity their subjects should follow. There was very little practice of toleration or freedom of worship, which meant that, in most countries, as in Bohemia, there were confessional groups who were marginalised or even persecuted.

But religious discord was only one cause of instability. We know from the trials and tribulations of the EU in the late twentieth century just how difficult it is for Europe's nations to live in harmony and pursue the common objectives of peace and economic prosperity. Four hundred years ago the situation was a lot worse. Since 1437 the continent had been dominated politically by the powerful Habsburg family. There were two branches. The Spanish Habsburgs ruled Spain, Portugal (till 1640), the southern Netherlands, bits of Italy and an extensive overseas empire. Their Austrian cousins became the hereditary rulers of the Holy Roman Empire. The imperial Crown theoretically imparted a measure of unity to central Europe, which, in the seventeenth century, was a hodge-podge of nationalities and more than thirty small German principalities and city states. However, the individual components of the empire enjoyed a large measure of autonomy, and the leading princes elected the emperor. Voltaire, the French philosopher, was quite right when he observed that this mélange of political units was 'neither holy, nor Roman nor an empire'. However, together with the land ruled by the Spanish Habsburgs, it was a real threat to

Europe's other major political power, France. The French felt pressured, hemmed in, denied living space.

All the elements were in place for a political meltdown and Ferdinand II was the man who turned up the heat of the furnace. One of his first acts on becoming emperor was to abolish all the rights enjoyed by his Protestant subjects in Austria. This zealot now embarked on what he considered was a holy war against heretics. After all, he reasoned, was the survival of his agents in Prague anything less than a divine miracle? He assembled an army to deal with the Bohemian rebels, aided by their Hungarian co-religionists. He won some early victories in the field. Had he stopped there,he might have got away with it but, believing himself to be on a roll and a holy roll at that, he issued, in 1628, the Edict of Restitution. This ordered that all lands taken from the Catholic Church over the last troubled century were to be restored. There were many Protestant princes who were not obsessively attached to their religious beliefs. But their property? That was a different matter. Moreover, some of the confiscated Church lands were now held by Catholic princes. Several of Ferdinand's wealthier subjects looked on apprehensively as his troops used disproportionate force to stamp his authority on those who questioned his policies. In Bohemia all the nobles lost their lands and many were executed. One historian described the nation as being 'decapitated'.

Fear now ruled the chancelleries of mainland northern Europe and indignation fired the resolve of rulers outside the immediate combat area. Other nations were drawn into the conflict. Some, like England, sent troops to fight for their co-religionists. The kings of Denmark and Sweden brought their own armies to the fray. France was hesitant about succouring Protestants but was worried about mounting Habsburg power and got round the problem by subsidising the Swedes. Many were the deals struck by kings, princes and city councils, each governed by self-interest. So, one way or another, the war – really a series of campaigns interspersed with brief periods of peace – dragged on from year to year.

The intervention of Sweden in 1630 marked a major turning point in the conflict. The king, Gustavus Adolphus, was a military genius and he was heftily backed by French gold to the tune of a million livres. He genuinely desired to come to the aid of the beleaguered Protestants, but he also intended to assert Sweden's commercial dominance in the Baltic by gaining territory along its southern shore. Up to this point events had been running the emperor's way, thanks largely to the activities of his talented generals, Albrecht von Wallenstein and Johann, Count Tilly. Most of the early fighting

occurred in northern Germany and, simultaneously, the Spanish Habsburgs were trying to crush
the Calvinist Dutch United Provinces. Gustavus
put a sharp end to their advance at the beginning of
1631. He drove an imperial army back to Frankfurt-
on-Oder, laid siege to it in April and wiped out the
enemy. But this did not clear his way to advance
against Tilly's main force which was engaged in
a siege of its own at Magdeburg, south-west of
Berlin.

This fine ancient city of 30,000 inhabitants
would be a crucial prize of war for three reasons:
it occupied a vital strategic position on the Elbe;
it was well stocked with food; and it was, by long
tradition, staunchly Lutheran and its capture would
therefore be a major psychological blow to the
enemy. But both the armies in northern Germany
had their problems. Tilly's men were suffering badly
from a shortage of supplies. The ravaged countryside
had little more it could provide and Tilly appealed
to his fellow general for aid but Wallenstein had
his own agenda and was more than content to sit
back, keeping his own troops fresh and watching
Tilly get into deeper and deeper difficulties. Not
for the first or last time in the annals of war, success
or failure was decided, not by the clash of enemies
but by the jealous rivalries of commanders on the
same side. There was no love lost between the two
generals; making life difficult for Tilly weighed

more heavily with Wallenstein than commitment to the common cause. On the other side, Gustavus was also having difficulties with men he had hoped would fight beside him. Some of the Protestant German princes, instead of looking upon the Swedish king as a deliverer, were suspicious of his territorial ambitions. They blocked his path while they tried to make peace with the emperor. All these personal animosities created a position of stalemate. The consequences would prove fatal to thousands of innocent Germans.

Strategic stalemate was one of the worst things that could happen in seventeenth-century warfare. Idle armies rapidly became demoralised. More than that, they became resentful. And hungry. The fighting units involved in the Thirty Years War were a mixed bunch. Most had a core of hardy, battle-toughened professionals, either royal guards or mercenaries. Their numbers were augmented by volunteers, who enlisted out of a thirst for adventure, or commitment to a religious or national cause, or the hope of booty. But the majority of soldiers were conscripts, men plucked from the plough or prison or the ranks of unemployed vagabonds. Such motley crews had little concern for 'rules of engagement'. Their first and most desperate need was to survive and they knew that their chances were slim. One Swedish village sent 230 men to the war between 1621 and 1639. Fifteen returned home, five of them cripples. That was far from an atypical community. Moreover, the age of conscription was lowered as the conflict dragged on. Those African child soldiers drafted into modern wars had their counterparts in Europe 400 years ago.

The stalemate came to an end on 14 May when the intransigent Ferdinand rejected the overtures of the Protestant princes, thus driving them into the arms of Gustavus. Unfortunately, it was too late to avoid tragedy. Gustavus was eager to draw the imperial army into a pitched battle over Magdeburg – where the people were desperately looking to the Swedes for relief – but he was still 240 kilometres away. As for Tilly's troops, they were hungry and weary and in no shape to face the enemy in open field. The citizens of Magdeburg looked fearfully from their walls at the encircling besiegers and scanned the horizon anxiously for a sight of Swedish banners. In these circumstances, Gustavus did the only thing in his power. He sent one of his officers, Dietrich von Falkenberg, to organise the city's defence and keep up public morale until he could arrive to relieve them. From other parts of Protestant Europe messages of support poured in. Bundles of pamphlets were distributed urging 'brave little Magdeburg' to stand firm.

Easy enough for outsiders to take such a positive stance! But it was not so easy for Magdeburg's inhabitants. In May 1631 the citizenry was divided.

Quarrels and fights between pro- and anti-Swedish factions were as bitter as the warfare outside the city walls. Falkenberg found it difficult to obtain food for his men because merchants hid their stores. If the siege was going to be protracted they saw their first priority as being to feed themselves and their neighbours. Falkenberg tried to steel the people's resistance by assuring them that his master was on the move.

Ironically, this rumour had an unfortunate and unforeseen effect. When it reached the ranks of the besiegers, it panicked them into redoubling their efforts. They knew they had to take the city and commandeer all the food they could lay their hands on as soon as possible if they were to be in any shape to face the advancing Swedes. They had become little more than crazed animals who would do whatever was necessary to ensure their survival. On 17 May Tilly's men began a fierce artillery bombardment. It went on, unsuccessfully, for more than two days. It was dawn on the 20th before a breach was, at last, made large enough for the desperate invaders to pour through. The defenders put up a good fight and Falkenberg, in the forefront of the battle, was cut down by enemy musket fire.

What followed was an orgy of killing, brutality, plunder and destruction on a scale that shocked the whole of Europe. Tilly's troops swept through the city, completely out of control, mindlessly punishing a defenceless civilian population for their own sufferings. They broke into wine cellars and rapidly got drunk. Now they were not only savage beasts; they were insensible savage beasts, slaughtering every cowering man, woman or child they came across. Tilly did what he could to alleviate the suffering. He was seen snatching a baby from the arms of its butchered mother. He had 600 women and children herded into the cathedral and placed a guard on the doors. Six hundred– but this out of a population of 30,000! Hardly an impressive example of clemency. The final death toll was of the order of 25,000.

It is almost with a sense of ghoulish satisfaction that we read what happened next. The conquerors gained little from their victory. At the beginning of the onslaught, they had set fire to one of the city gates to stop it being closed again. Whether windblown sparks carried to the thatched roofs and timber-framed houses of the crammed streets or whether defiant citizens deliberately fired the city to deny the imperialists their triumph, we will never know. What we do know is that beautiful Magdeburg was soon in flames from one end to the other. The pile of smouldering ash took days to cool down and when it did the gaunt, blackened walls of the cathedral and a handful of other churches and public buildings stood like tombstones in a bleak, grey landscape. The city had to be rebuilt almost from scratch. It survived until 1945, only to be flattened again by Allied bombing. Whoever was responsible for the destruction caused by the inferno, the immediate impact on Tilly's army was catastrophic. They were able to salvage little from the burning city to satiate their hunger and fortify them to continue the war.

Tilly does not come across as a vicious man and he certainly was not an ineffective commander. But the depressing aftermath of the devastation imposed a severe burden with which he found it difficult to cope. Not only did he have to restore order among his reeling soldiery and somehow find means of feeding them, he also had a refugee problem on his hands. He ordered the surviving citizens to be lodged in the roofless cloister of a ruined monastery. There they huddled under blankets and, one by one, died of starvation. This added the threat of disease to the hardships of the imperial troops. They simply could not cope with the enormous number of burials. Eventually Tilly ordered all the remaining corpses to be thrown into the Elbe. For months afterwards the river was choked with putrid bodies. The general was badly shaken by the disaster at Magdeburg. It took him several days to get a grip on the situation and pluck some shreds of honour from his unfortunate 'victory'. He made a great show of a rededication ceremony in the cathedral. All elements of Protestantism were purged and the building was consecrated to the Virgin Mary. He ordered that the name 'Magdeburg' should be obliterated, along with most of the city itself. Henceforth it was to be known as 'Marienburg'. It was an empty gesture. Months later, when the last occupying troops marched out through the broken gate towers, having started fresh fires in order to render the city utterly useless to their enemies, the remnant citizens crawled from their cellars and blackened refuges and repudiated the name bestowed upon their city in its baptism of fire.

If Magdeburg was a disaster to both its defenders and attackers, it was a total calamity for the imperial cause. Tilly wearily informed his superiors, 'Our danger has no end, for the Protestant Estates will without doubt be only strengthened in their hatred.' He himself was henceforth known as the Butcher of Magdeburg and 'to magdeburg' was coined as a verb signifying barbarian brutality. News of the Protestant 'martyrs' of Magdeburg spread rapidly throughout Europe. No less than 246 pamphlets and broadsides were distributed, denouncing Ferdinand and warning his non-Catholic subjects what they could expect at his hands. Fear now gripped the inhabitants on both sides of the battle zone. The ghost of Magdeburg threatened Protestant and Catholic alike. For, if in the future a Catholic city should fall to a Protestant army, what quarter could its citizens expect from the vengeful foe?

As for Gustavus, the loss of this one city was not the catastrophe that it might have seemed: indeed, it was to prove incalculably more valuable than any victory he might have won over Tilly in the field. For the north German princes now had no alternative but to throw in their lot with him. Moreover, the Dutch United Provinces voted to provide a considerable sum to support the Protestant champion.

The allied force the Swedish king could muster numbered well over 40,000 and he, at last, had freedom to move his host through the lands of his new allies. Even with fresh draftees Tilly could not put more than 30,000 men in the field, but there was no way he could delay an encounter. The powerful alliance now formed against him left him little room for manoeuvre. When he threatened the ruler of Saxony with severe reprisals if he refused to give the emperor's men free passage, back came the defiant answer: 'I see that the Saxon sweetmeats, so long spared, are to be eaten but you may find that they contain hard nuts that will break your teeth.' For weeks Tilly marched his army to and fro, desperately pillaging villages and homesteads for the newly harvested grain and the season's livestock required to sustain his men and horses. Still he looked in vain to Wallenstein for supplies. Still he hoped in vain to receive reinforcements from the emperor. His wanderings came to an end in mid-September.

The two armies met outside the village of Breitenfeld, north of Leipzig, on the 18th. It was an afternoon of high heat and swirling dust. Through the haze Tilly beheld an unfamiliar sight. Instead of being confronted with a traditional battle formation – massed infantry in the centre, flanked by cavalry on both wings – he saw that Gustavus had deployed his forces very differently. The Swedish king had arranged his cavalry in squares. Between them he had placed files of musketeers. The latter stood in files of five, one behind another. The front man adopted a kneeling position so that he and the soldier behind could fire simultaneously. As soon as they had discharged their weapons they retreated to the back of the column to reload and the next pair took their places. The Swedes were thus able to keep up an unrelenting fire, while the loose cavalry formation allowed the horsemen greater freedom of movement than the conventional line abreast. Any damage done by enemy cannon did not open up a serious breach in their ranks. Tilly's cavalry charged and charged again. His artillery pounded the Swedish ranks. But Gustavus's men stood their ground. After two hours the imperialists broke themselves against the rock-like Swedish squares. Although the Swede's Saxon allies were driven from the field, the imperialists were unable to create a tactical advantage. As the day lengthened it seemed that nothing could break the stalemate.

In that age battles were not infrequently decided by the caprices of the weather. So it was on this occasion. A change of wind direction blew clouds of choking dust into the faces of Tilly's weary troops. Blinded and confused by the fog-like haze, they faltered and, at last, turned to flee. They left over 7,000 of their comrades strewn across the battlefield of Breitenfeld. More were cut down in the ensuing pursuit or hastened to surrender. In all, Tilly lost two-thirds of his force. Protestant Europe was of course cock-a-hoop at this first victory over a large imperial army. But the man who derived the greatest satisfaction from it was Albrecht Wenzel von Wallenstein, Tilly's old military rival.

The man to whom I have so far made only passing reference was one of the most sinister figures of the age. His career illustrates beautifully the extent to which ambition and greed, allied to contempt for the claims of loyalty and supreme indifference to human suffering, play lead roles in most military confrontations. Born in 1583 in the Bohemian town of Heřmanice into a Protestant family, Wallenstein converted to Catholicism, married a rich widow and used her fortune to ingratiate himself with Ferdinand II. He raised a mercenary army, proved himself to be a first-rate military commander and won the gratitude of his master. Ferdinand was generous in rewarding his general and lavished lands, titles and other perks upon him. By 1625 Wallenstein had become Duke of Friedland and Governor of Bohemia. His business acumen was as acute as his tactical skill. When his first wife died, he lost no time in making a second, even more advantageous marriage. His bride was Isabella von Harrach, daughter of the emperor's closest confidant.

When, in 1625, the Thirty Years War reached a critical phase, Wallenstein offered to raise a private army for the emperor. Ferdinand should have been cautious about accepting. The existence of a wealthy, independent prince commanding an army loyal to himself alone might have worried a more far-seeing ruler. But Ferdinand trusted his general and was ready to use any means to crush the damnable Protestant heretics. Wallenstein had been largely responsible for the early imperialist successes. Four remarkable years of campaigning had made him master of northern Germany, and a grateful emperor bestowed upon him the hereditary dukedom of Mecklenburg. Wallenstein's ambition now soared. He saw himself as an equal of the emperor and set about his own diplomatic negotiations with the Catholic and Protestant rulers of Europe. In 1630 Ferdinand was obliged to sack him.

That proved to be as big a mistake as hiring him. Wallenstein was bent on revenge and also intended to play the role of an independent warlord, switching allegiances from side to side in pursuit of purely personal advantage. When Gustavus Adolphus entered the fray, Wallenstein had offered him an alliance, but the Swedish king was more canny than the emperor, and refused to trust a man who had turned his religious coat. Piqued, the duke now withdrew from the fray altogether and took his personal army with him. He would show the generalissimos that they could not wage war without him. This was why he refused aid to the desperate General Tilly. Had he behaved differently, the outcome of Breitenfeld would have been very different.

After that battle Wallenstein had Ferdinand over a barrel. He was the only general who could stop Gustavus and he knew it. All central Europe lay open to the Swedish king. There was little to stop Gustavus marching south – towards Vienna, the imperial capital. Feeling he had no alternative, the emperor offered to reinstate his commander, but Wallenstein was determined to make his former boss grovel. The terms he demanded were exorbitant: supreme command of all imperial forces, complete freedom of diplomatic negotiation and personal promotion as a prince of the empire with further grants of land to support his dignity. Ferdinand had to accept the humiliation of being dictated to by one of his own subjects.

Meanwhile, Gustavus was inexorably on the march. Major centres of European civilisation fell to his army or joyfully welcomed their deliverance from imperial rule. Nuremberg, Ingolstadt, Augsburg, Munich – all were in his hands by the spring of 1632. He boasted that in three weeks he would march his army through the streets of the imperial capital. Tilly tried to prevent him crossing the River Lech near its junction with the Danube but the Swedish juggernaut was unstoppable. During the fray the Butcher of Magdeburg was shot in the leg and within days he was dead. This was the background to Ferdinand's desperate bargaining with Wallenstein.

Wallenstein's first task was to slow down Gustavus's approach. He fortified a strong castle near Nuremberg, thus threatening to retake this important city. Gustavus could not leave such a stronghold in his rear and had to spend weeks in a fruitless siege. Eventually, with the campaigning season drawing to its end, both commanders withdrew their forces. Having been plundered by two armies, the local people were left to face the onset of winter with their larders empty. 'For three months we were besieged by our enemies,' one Nuremberger complained, 'and for four months were eaten out of house and home by our friends.' When Gustavus visited Wallenstein's deserted garrison, he discovered hundreds of wounded imperial troops who were too weak to march with their army and had been left to crawl among the corpses of dead comrades and horses, searching for water and any scraps of whatever might pass for food.

But Wallenstein had been mistaken in assuming that fighting was over for the year. When Gustavus learned that his enemy was withdrawing into winter quarters, he hastened in pursuit. The two great generals confronted each other for the first – and last – time near the small town of Lützen, south-west of Leipzig, on 16 November 1632. All day long battle raged back and forth, through mist and gunsmoke, which drifted in obscuring clouds across the sodden fields. In the melee confusion reigned. No one could tell how the day went. Rumour spread on both sides that Gustavus had been killed, but there was no let-up in the furious assault offered by his men. Wallenstein's second-in-command was certainly slain and the general himself was in excruciating pain from gout. As soon as darkness fell he called off his men and retreated, leaving all his artillery and baggage train and another 6,000 dead soldiers in the trampled mud. A furious Wallenstein refused to accept personal responsibility for the defeat. He had seventeen officers shot for cowardice and put a price on the heads of forty more who had fled.

However, the imperial general did have a large consolation prize. The rumours of Gustavus's death were true. His body was discovered by Swedish troops as they were clearing the battlefield. It lay beneath a pile of corpses and was scarred with numerous wounds, including one that has ever after raised the suspicion of treachery – the king had a bullet hole in his back. The great Swedish adventure was over. The king's army withdrew and took no further part in the war. The map of Europe that had, briefly, been redrawn resumed much of its former shape. All the contenders were exhausted and ready to come together to agree a temporary peace on terms that they could probably have agreed before all the carnage started. Then, in 1635, France entered directly into the war and the sorry tale began all over again.

The cost of the 1631–2 campaigns far exceeded the thousands of combatants killed or maimed in battle. Neither statistics nor anecdotal evidence can begin to convey the horrors suffered by all those who lived within reach of the tide of war. The historian C.V. Wedgwood provides us with just a whiff of that horror:

The Alsatian town of Hagenau, three times occupied in eighteen months, lamented: 'We have had blue-coats and red-coats and now come the yellow-coats. God have pity on us.' At Frankfurt-on-the-Oder pestilence bred of the rotting bodies of the dead had overwhelmed the survivors. At Stettin and Spandau the Swedes had left the plague, in the towns of Durlach and Lorch, at Würzburg and in the whole province of Württemberg; at Bamberg the bodies lay unburied in the streets, and on both banks of the Rhine there was famine, so that the peasants from miles around came in to Mainz to work on the fortifications for a little bread. The harvest of 1632 promised well, but in Bavaria and Swabia the passing troops trampled it down; in Bavaria there was neither corn left to grind nor seed to sow for the year to come; plague and famine wiped out whole villages, mad dogs attacked their masters, and the authorities posted men with guns to shoot down the raving victims before they could contaminate their fellows; hungry wolves abandoned the woods and mountains to roam through the deserted hamlets, devouring the dying and the dead.

The Swedish army alone destroyed 1,500 German towns, 18,000 villages and 2,000 castles.

In the light of such suffering it seems almost obscenely irrelevant to record the fate of the remaining major players in the events of 1631–2. The Emperor Ferdinand II died in his bed in 1637, two years after having to compromise with the Protestant princes at the Peace of Prague. His great Catholic crusade had failed but this did not prevent him being revered as a great champion of the faith. Ferdinand's God was obviously one who revelled in bloodshed. And Wallenstein? His arrogance and cynical coat-turning received its appropriate reward in 1634. Ferdinand, driven to desperate measures, issued a contract against his own general. Wallenstein and his immediate entourage were stabbed to death by British mercenaries in Ferdinand's pay.

In the eighteenth century partisan historians – interested in portraying the Thirty Years War as a brave Protestant struggle against Catholic tyranny, or a holy Catholic crusade against heretics and rebels – called the conflict the last of Europe's wars of religion. After 1648, many claimed, kings and governments threw off all pretence of Christian ideology and pursued naked territorialism and political power in their struggles with each other. This way of thinking is based on a double fallacy. One is that wars are occasional interruptions to essentially peaceful international relations. The other is that, in any society that calls itself civilised, there is no necessity for leaders to justify starting wars.

Warfare is the perpetual fate of humanity and peace is an illusion. Think of the twentieth century. Europe was at war – whether 'hot' or 'cold' – from 1914 to 1990. And when the continent itself was not embroiled in bloodshed, many of its younger citizens were involved in conflicts elsewhere – Algeria, Congo, Kenya, Egypt, Lebanon, Syria, India, Malaysia, Cambodia, to mention but a few. Since 1990 we have been sending our young men and women to risk their lives in Kuwait, Iraq and Afghanistan. Why? Because war, it seems, is what human beings do. And they do it in many different ways. The bloody horrors of 1631–2 provide us with excellent examples of different kinds of warmongers.

There is something rather chilling about the Emperor Ferdinand II. In his personal life he was charming and self-effacing and there was no suggestion of cruelty about his dealings with others. He was a stranger to violence and never ventured anywhere near a battlefield. How was it, then, that this avuncular ruler could unleash on his own people death and destruction of biblical proportions? The answer lies in the two causes that he convinced himself were important above all others. One was the preservation of the Holy Roman Empire. He had received it as a solemn charge and felt honour bound to pass it on intact to his successor. The integrity of this strange conglomeration of central European states was very much under threat when Ferdinand assumed control. The tensions caused by nationalism and religion seemed poised to tear the ancient institution apart. In 1618 he did not for a moment question that the Bohemian rebellion had to be crushed. Ferdinand's second conviction was that Catholicism was the only glue that could hold together the fragments of the empire. More than that it was The Truth. If ever the emperor, confronted with the sufferings his armies were inflicting on non-combatants, wavered in his determination, the Jesuit priests who were the guardians of his conscience were on hand to remind him of his divine mission. They must certainly share the blood-guilt that was Ferdinand's.

Albrecht Wenzel von Wallenstein was very different. He did not live in some palace remote from the action, fawned upon by sycophantic courtiers. He did not trouble himself with ideology. He was a pragmatist who knew the realities of war at first hand and calculated how they could be best turned to his own advantage. If he had belief in anything beyond his own aggrandisement, it was in administrative efficiency. He had nothing but contempt for the emperor and those princes who lived remote from their people. Just as he cared for the well-being of his soldiers, so he was concerned for the material welfare of his subjects. He could never understand that some people were motivated by higher considerations of loyalty or religion. If men like Ferdinand and Gustavus were blinkered by genuine beliefs, Wallenstein was equally hampered by a complete lack of faith (except in himself). It was his misreading of the loyalty of imperial officers that brought about his own bloody end.

Gustavus Adolphus claimed that his motive for involvement in the affairs of central Europe was mainly defensive. Sweden was heavily reliant on trade through the Baltic and this depended on maintaining good contacts with its German trading partners. Relations with Denmark were bad after a recent war which had ended disastrously for Sweden, hampering its access to the North Sea and the leading mercantile nations of Holland and England. If the emperor were to extend his power over the Lutheran states of northern Germany, Sweden's commercial situation could only become worse. The nation would be hemmed in by potential enemies. There was even the possibility that Ferdinand might use the southern Baltic as a base for a Catholic crusade. Do we believe Gustavus's stated reasons? Was his claim to be fighting a war only for the survival of his country simply a smoke-screen for territorial ambition? Was Gustavus using the '*lebesraum*' ('living space') argument that Adolf Hitler produced in the 1930s to justify his expansionism? Some of the German princes this 'Lion of the North' came to 'help' undoubtedly believed that Gustavus was interested only in gaining permanent bases on the southern Baltic shore. It was their refusal to cooperate that slowed down the king's advance and led to the fall of Magdeburg. It is certainly true that, by the end of the war, Sweden had gained possessions on the other side of the sea. Once he had landed on German soil with an army that was second to none in Europe, he needed powerful arguments to justify his march across the continent. It was then that he put himself at the head of a Protestant league aimed at guaranteeing religious toleration for his allies. He became, and has remained in legend ever since, the great Protestant champion. Was he a man of principle, prepared to live, fight and die for the greater good? Did those who perished alongside him believe that they were sacrificing themselves to make a better world? These are questions we need to ask about the politicians and generals of past centuries – and, even more, about our own leaders.

In 1648 the exhausted combatants agreed terms in the Peace of Westphalia. The principal players did not live to see it. They had all been consumed by the greedy monster that is war. Even though Ferdinand had made a peaceful end, his death, at fifty-nine, was hastened by the rigid work regime and the religious austerities he imposed upon himself. Did those who took up the batons set themselves to create a better world? Did they hopefully refer to the horrors of 1618–48 as the 'war to end all wars'? Hardly. Ferdinand III proved to be as zealous as his father. He called into being a standing army to police his dominions more effectively. Pope Innocent X was furious that the anti-Protestant crusade had been called off. He denounced the peace treaty as 'null, void, invalid, iniquitous, unjust, damnable, reprobate, inane, empty of meaning and effect for all time'. In 1655 the Empire and Sweden were once more at war (together with Poland, Denmark, Brandenburg and the United Netherlands). In 1685 it was the turn of Louis XIV of France to instigate a widespread persecution of French Protestants, thousands of whom fled abroad. Did the Thirty Years War decide anything? To quote C.V. Wedgwood again: 'Morally subversive, economically destructive, socially degrading, confused in its causes, devious in its course, futile in its results, it is the outstanding example in European history of meaningless conflict.'

Chapter 5

1709

We experienced such cold as I shall never forget. The spittle from mouths turned to ice before it reached the ground, sparrows fell frozen from roofs to the ground. You could see some men without hands and feet, others deprived of fingers, face, ears and noses, others crawling like quadrupeds.

Such were the recollections of a chaplain serving with what had been the finest army in Europe during the winter of 1709. The Swedish army, under the command of the young King Charles XII, was widely acknowledged as the best-trained, best-equipped and best-disciplined military force that had existed in Europe for a very long time. By the summer of 1708 Charles was ready for a showdown with Peter I, the barbaric ruler of Russia who had presumed to challenge Sweden's command of the Baltic. He was about to pit his magnificent fighting machine against Peter's army of half-trained peasants. It was, as one English commentator observed, an army of veterans facing a mob. Charles's contest with Peter and his allies had, in fact, been under way for nine years and, in virtually every encounter, the Swedes had whipped the pants off their opponents. But Charles had never been able to bring his enemy to face him in a major battle. That was about to change. He was now all set to take the war into Russia and deliver the *coup de grâce*. His foe would be forced to stand and fight. Failure to do so would simply leave open the door to Moscow.

Charles's strategy was straightforward. He had 35,000 men under his command when he reached the River Dnieper. At Riga (capital of Latvia) on the Baltic Coast his general, Count Adam Löwenhaupt, was stationed with another 12,500 troops and wagons loaded with vital supplies. When these arrived Charles would be ready to cross the Russian frontier and strike north-eastwards towards Moscow, 800 kilometres away. Before the autumn set in he would have brought the Russian tsar to his knees. There could be no question of venturing into enemy territory until he had the fresh troops, food and equipment his subordinate was bringing. But Löwenhaupt was expected every day. He did not arrive. His start had been delayed by difficulties in commandeering horses. Fortunately Charles did have a plan B. He had formed an alliance with the Cossack chief, Mazeppa, whose territory lay farther south in the grain-rich Ukraine. Clearly the invasion would have to be postponed until the next campaign season. Until then Charles had a choice of strategies: he could either set up camp for the winter where he was and wait for Löwenhaupt or march his men to the Ukraine. He decided on the latter course. Too late he learned that both Mazeppa and Löwenhaupt had met with Russian attacks and been badly mauled. There would be no immediate relief for Charles's hungry men. By this time the Swedes had reached an area to the east of Kiev. There was no option but to dig in where they were to see out the winter.

For a disciplined army like the Swedes that would not have been a major problem – under normal circumstances. But the winter of 1708–9 was very far from normal. In fact, it was the coldest and the longest for more than 200 years (and, very probably, for much longer still). In Paris on 14 January a temperature of minus fifteen degrees centigrade was recorded. In London the thermometer recorded minus twelve (the recommended temperature for a modern domestic freezer is minus eighteen). Average temperatures throughout Europe were seven degrees centigrade below normal. Rivers iced over, coastal waters froze from the Baltic to the Adriatic. Venetians were able to walk across their lagoon. The earth became like iron to a depth of more than a metre. Autumn-sown crops perished. Fish died in their ponds, cattle in their byres, birds fell from the sky, wild animals collapsed with hypothermia and starvation, mature trees exploded as their sap froze solid. Nor was this frightening phenomenon a mere cold snap: the great freeze began around the turn of the year and, with only a brief intermission, continued until the end of March.

When nature 'breaks the rules' so dramatically, human suffering reaches new depths. No houses, not even the palaces of the wealthy, were equipped to cope with such fierce cold. The Duchess of Orleans wrote from luxurious Versailles to a relative: 'I am sitting by a roaring fire, have a screen before the door, which is closed, so that I can sit here with a sable fur piece around my neck and my feet in a bearskin sack and I am still shivering with cold and can barely hold the pen'. She was one of the lucky ones. In villages throughout Europe people huddled around bonfires, which were kept burning perpetually as long as branches, seasoned timber or even furniture could be found to feed the flames. English sailors aboard a man-o-war in an Italian harbour died in their cots.

One observer reckoned that 'the great frost was most severely felt in France, where in most places the fruit trees were killed, and the corn frozen to the ground, which occasioned there a dreadful calamity and desolation'. As Europe's principal wine producer, France was, inevitably, hit very badly when millions of vines were destroyed. The national economy and the livelihoods of thousands of vineyard owners and workers were shattered and it took several years for fresh stock to be planted and matured to the point where production could recover its pre-Great Freeze levels. But there was one important French export that never recovered. A species of tree that suffered particularly badly in France was the walnut, known by cabinetmakers as 'Grenoble wood'. Among wealthy patrons in late-seventeenth-/early-eighteenth-century society, furniture made of, or veneered in, walnut was greatly prized. To own cabinets surfaced in this wood with its beautifully patterned grain – 'very black in colour and so admirably streaked, as to represent natural flowers, landskips and other fancies' – was the height of fashion. Walnut fuelled a major native furniture industry and was an important timber export. In 1720 that export was banned as the stocks of seasoned timber dwindled. It would be almost a century before new trees would reach the maturity to be felled and so provide fresh stocks of wood.

By the time that happened fashion had passed on from what furniture historians call the 'age of walnut'. Cabinetmakers had been obliged to look elsewhere for their timber. A writer in 1786 informed his readers:

Formerly the walnut tree was propagated for its wood but since the importation of mahogany and the Virginia walnut it has considerably decreased in reputation.

Europe began to look to the colonies to make good the deficiency in native timber. Initially this gave a boost to the economy of Virginia, where a related species of walnut grew in abundance. But the real winners were the plantation owners of Jamaica, Cuba and Honduras, who filled the gap in the market with mahogany. Fashion was quick to make a virtue of necessity. By the mid-1720s the 'new look' was the lustrous deep reddish-brown of the exotic tropical timber that would never grow in Europe. The 'age of mahogany' had arrived. And the deforestation of large areas of the Caribbean began. This very dense wood had, according to the salesmen, uses far beyond the decoration of the homes of the wealthy:

> The excellence of this wood for all domestic uses is now sufficiently known… it is in no less esteem for shipbuilding, having properties for that use excelling oak and all other wood.

This change in public taste was directly due to the appalling winter of 1709. But the same circumstances that provided a challenge to craftsmen, and an opportunity to the owners of town and country mansions to exhibit the new 'cool', were a matter of life and death to the majority of peasant farmers who, at the best of times, lived not far above the level of subsistence. We are all familiar with the images of drought-parched lands in Africa with their skeletal inhabitants forced to rely on foreign aid. Such extreme weather has only very rarely occurred in the temperate lands of Europe, but it did appear in 1709.

> What hope was there for individual citizens? Their heart-rending lamentations filled the listening air and existence seemed only possible in another clime and other new conditions.

If that contemporary account seems to us a bit OTT, we have only to call to mind the wailing women of disaster zones pictured on our TV screens as they bury their children or raise their despairing cries over the graves of their husbands. At least French countrymen in the summer of 1709 could go out into the fields, get down on all fours and eat grass like sheep. Many did just that. The same chronicler went on to describe one concomitant of the Great Freeze with which we, too, are depressingly familiar:

> To make matters worse, even in that time of dire distress, speculators came to the front, bought the grain that frugal farmers had saved and sought to

make a profit even out of famine. Nor could all the efforts on the part of the government check it.

It was not only country-dwellers who suffered. The few available supplies could not reach the major centres of population because roads and rivers were blocked by snow and ice. The city of Paris was effectively cut off from the outside world for three months. And it was not alone. When the wagons, ships and river barges did begin to move again, they had little relief to bring to the clamouring citizenry. The summer and autumn brought only the most meagre yields of grain, fruit and olives. People made 'bread' from ground ferns, nettles and thistles. The government, with good reason, feared street riots. To avert revolution they forced the wealthy to open their larders, dole out food at their gates and set up soup kitchens.

If life was terrible for ordinary French people in the year 1709, for the Swedish soldiers trapped on Russia's western border it was a living hell. The land was soon scavenged dry. Parties sent farther afield in search of food ran the risk of being picked off by Russian patrols. The soliders needed to build up their bodies in order to survive the appalling climatic conditions, but had to exist on the most meagre rations. Those who managed to commandeer space in a ruined cottage or a barn were the lucky ones. The rest made do as best they could.

They had an inadequate supply of tents and, in any case, these provided no insulation against the bitter winds and the frequent blizzards. Some of Charles's men could do no better for themselves than crouch against walls, or huddle together in trenches gouged out of the iron earth. Thousands succumbed to frostbite, hypothermia and malnutrition. By the time winter relaxed its hold on the earth, half of the Swedish army was dead. Tsar Peter's men, of course, had to endure the same weather, but they had secure supply lines and could build themselves suitable shelters.

As the weather eased, prudence might have suggested that Charles should withdraw westwards, await reinforcements and allow his surviving troops to recover completely. But the Swedish king was determined not to relax his pressure on the Russians. Although his army was now greatly outnumbered and his enemy was fighting on his own ground, Charles still believed he could dispose of the barbarian menace in one pitched battle. The result was the Battle of Poltava (27 June 1709), one of the major turning points in European history – and, indeed, in world history. When news of it reached London, the novelist and leading man of letters, Daniel Defoe, described it as 'an army of veterans defeated by a mob, a crowd, a mere militia; an army of the bravest fellows in the world beaten by scoundrels'. Charles XII was certainly not defeated by any superior generalship on the part of Tsar Peter, nor by the superior fighting abilities of the Russians. Poltava was not a 'great battle' in any tactical sense. Peter established a strong defensive position and allowed the Swedish army to dash itself to pieces against his wooden palisade and the musket fire of his troops. Had the Swedes not been weakened by their privation or lack of supplies, they would, in all likelihood, have been able to prevail or at least withdraw in good order. As it was, they finally fled, leaving behind 10,000 dead, wounded or prisoner.

The Battle of Poltava ushered onto the stage of European affairs a nation hitherto regarded as a backward Asiatic people ruled by an uncouth tyrant. Ever since that day in June 1709, Russia has held a leading position among the world's major powers. The history books never fail to point this out. What they often omit to mention is that the victory that transformed the fate of the nation was, in large measure, due to climatic conditions beyond the powers of any human monarch or general to control.

These very conditions were, at the same time, creating problems for the government in distant London. During the months of May and June 1709, the citizens of the city of London were astonished to find the streets of that metropolis swarming with men and women of an alien race, speaking an unknown tongue and bearing unmistakable indications of poverty, misery and want. It soon became known that about 5,000 of these people were sheltered under tents in the suburbs of the city. Additions were almost daily made to their number during June, July, August and September, and by October between 13,000 and 14,000 had come.

This unprecedented influx of destitute refugees came from an area of the German Rhineland between Cologne and Mannheim. For eight years these people from the cockpit of Europe had suffered as armies fighting the War of the Spanish Succession had advanced and retreated over their lands, trampling their crops, requisitioning their livestock, raping their daughters and firing their barns. All this they had been able to endure because the tide of war rolled on; the battalions moved out in search of new battlegrounds; there had been time to repair damaged buildings, plant the new season's crops and, if necessary, start again from scratch. Humble German farmers were resilient and used to hardship. But the past winter had broken their spirit. Now, it seemed, the very fields worked by the same families for generations had turned against them. The ground was unworkable. No ploughshare could turn it – always supposing that horses had survived to pull the ploughs. One eyewitness to the misery of the people wrote:

The pen almost refuses to do its task when asked to tell of the hundreds of strong men who, during that memorable winter, lay down to die of cold and hunger in the once fruitful valley of the Rhine. So intense was the cold that even the wild animals of the forest and the birds of the air were frozen to death. Wine was frozen in the casks and bottles. The vineyards were frozen to the ground and the fruit trees completely destroyed.

The Great Freeze had started the previous Christmas Eve with massive falls of snow. Unlike other winters with reflected sunshine glaring from the white landscape and glistening on icicles, this one was dark and drear. For three months grey cloud overshadowed all, occasionally tipping more snow onto earlier deposits, which were encrusted with centimetres-thick ice. Most farmers would have had supplies of meat and fish salted down for the winter and grain to feed the next season's breeding stock. But now there was not going to be a next season. They had to slaughter and eat the young animals to keep them from dying in misery. They had to use up or sell the seedcorn because the planting time came and went but the soil remained like granite. The savage winter had robbed farming communities of their future. Famine loomed, as those who did not leave in the first wave of emigration soon discovered. Over much of Europe the 1709 harvests were virtually non-existent. Nor was it only the workers on the land who suffered. Since agriculture was the economic basis of society, commercial intercourse ground to a halt, as another observer reported:

> Nobody could pay any more, because nobody was paid. The people of the country in consequence of exactions had become insolvent; commerce dried up and brought no returns. Good faith and confidence were abolished. Chaos, ruin and universal suffering prevailed.

There are very few situations in life so thoroughly negative that nobody wins. The desire of people to escape from the Rhineland was a godsend to property speculators. Never was land so cheap. Capitalists with the necessary resources to play the long game bought farms and holdings at a fraction of their normal value, knowing that they would be able to sell at huge profit when normal conditions returned.

Thousands of individuals and families were, therefore, on the move. They congregated in Holland but their destination was England, that traditional refuge of displaced persons from the Huguenots of the sixteenth century to the EU migrants of the twenty-first. Some of the Germans hoped to find in the island a new home and a fresh start. Others did not look that far ahead. They were driven by the imperative of the moment, believing only that whatever lay ahead could not be worse than what they were leaving behind. Then there were those who saw Queen Anne's realm as a staging post to the New World. For several decades groups of émigrés had made their way to the colonies of the Americas. The most attractive state to Germans contemplating crossing the Atlantic was Pennsylvania because it had a liberal constitution, was growing rapidly and was, around the turn of the eighteenth century, the most successful colony on the eastern seaboard. But to make such a huge move required organisation, money and the chartering of ships. Thus, the desperate travellers made first for England, with mixed hopes and plans. For the moment all they sought was employment, the chance to earn money to feed their families and, perhaps, to save enough to enable them, in the fullness of time, to move on.

Mass immigration is an alarming phenomenon and people respond in a variety of ways. Humanitarian feelings come up against economic realities and sheer racial prejudice. On 20 April 1968, the Conservative MP Enoch Powell delivered a speech about a problem that was then facing Britain. His words have achieved a lasting notoriety.

There are among the Commonwealth immigrants who have come to live here in the last fifteen years or so many thousands whose will and purpose is to be integrated… But to imagine that such a thing enters the heads of a great and growing majority of immigrants and their descendants is a ludicrous misconception, and a dangerous one. We are on the verge here of a change… As I look ahead I am filled with foreboding; like the Roman, I seem to see 'the River Tiber foaming with much blood'.

Such alarmist rhetoric raised enormous pro and anti responses from reactionaries and liberals at the time. In recent years similar prejudices have been stirred up by immigrants coming into Britain from EU countries. These instances may help us to understand the reactions of English or Dutch citizens to thousands of destitute Germans fleeing from the results of the Great Freeze and turning up on their doorsteps. There was a natural sympathy for these people, forced from their homes against their will. The good folk of several Dutch cities put their hands in their purses to help. They wanted to see the newcomers settled, but 'not in my back yard'. In April the burgomasters of Rotterdam authorised the distribution of money to the poverty-stricken Germans – not to relieve their immediate suffering but to help them on their way to England. The trouble was that that policy simply encouraged more refugees to make the journey. The Rhinelanders kept on coming, and kept on accepting the Dutch handouts. Enough was enough. On 12 August the city fathers issued a total prohibition on any further influx. They might as well have ordered a high North Sea tide not to overflow their dykes. Desperate people who could not turn back found numerous ways of infiltrating Holland. Like the determined young men who, in recent years, have besieged the ports of France in order to stow away in container lorries, these eighteenth-century seekers of a better life used ingenuity and ran grave risks to reach that horizon beyond which, they believed, lay a brighter future. River barges were set to patrol the Waal and the Maas to halt any immigrants they found. By late August they had already turned back over a thousand.

In Britain there was a similar pattern of response; initial sympathy and support was superseded by reluctance and firm prohibition. In the spring the House of Commons addressed the problem. Members were told that Queen Anne herself was moved by the plight of these poor people. As a result funds were raised to bring over 5,000 German immigrants. Thus the tented camps in the suburbs. But, by June, the temporary accommodation was bulging at the seams. Twice as many poor strangers were dwelling in the environs of the city as had been bargained for. Shanty towns grew up with the inevitable sights, sounds and smells always attendant upon overcrowded, unsanitary human agglomerations. The government was under pressure to 'do something', to get rid of the 'dirty foreigners'. There were protests, scuffles, mini-riots. Ministers did two things. They sent urgent orders to Mr Dayrolles, the English minister at The Hague. No more migrants could be accepted until satisfactory permanent provision had been made for those who had already arrived. The order had little effect. Poor people were still finding their way across the North Sea, often because they were surreptitiously being helped by the Dutch authorities to continue their journey. Since they could not reverse the tide, the best thing to do was help it on its way. When the English government protested through diplomatic channels, they received the vague response that the Dutch would 'make their best endeavours' to stem the flow. The other official action taken was to arrange passages for the unwelcome guests to those overseas places where few British citizens could be persuaded to go. The West Indies were short of minor officials and craftsmen. There was always room in Ireland for Protestant settlers to help keep the Catholic majority in order, and most of the Rhinelanders were Protestants. Getting immigrants to do jobs that indigenous people don't want to do is nothing new.

Some of the refugees fared better than those sent to the fever-ridden Caribbean or the remoter parts of Ireland. Those who had capital and/or contacts made good their original intention of heading for the east coast of North America. Some were assisted by the energetic recruiting activities of Benjamin Furley. This Quaker businessman who had settled in Rotterdam was a friend and associate of George Fox and William Penn, who were working hard to develop Pennsylvania. Land in the colony was available at knock-down prices and Furley offered additional cash inducements for families and individuals willing to make their home on the far side of the Atlantic.

It is only fair to point out that in 1709 Holland and Britain had reason for not wanting thousands of extra mouths to feed. The Great Freeze affected these countries too. The harvests were the worst in living memory. The prices of farm produce soared. Extra demand created by the immigrants sent them even higher. So the refugees were moved on – willingly or unwillingly.

But this did not entirely solve the problem. On the last day of 1709, the British government issued the following statement:

> Inasmuch as during the summer just past a number of poor people arrived here in England, from different parts of Germany, who have hitherto been supported by Her Royal Majesty, and have gradually been sent to the West Indies, and afterwards to

Ireland: and whereas more such poor people have come here since, notice has consequently been sent to Holland and elsewhere that none such would be passed, much less supported, and that those who have arrived here since the first of last October were to be sent back to Germany via Holland at the first opportunity. All such as intend to come hither are therefore notified to desist from their voyage which would assuredly result in failure unless it be that they have means of their own with which to support themselves.

But any stemming of the flow that such directives might have succeeded in achieving was only of a temporary nature. What began in 1709 was one of the most significant migrations in Western history. Throughout the ensuing decades over 100,000 men, women and children would leave Germany to become settlers in overseas territories ruled by other nations.

If you read the standard history books you will discover that in 1709 the 'Ancien Régime' in Europe, the system of rule by absolute monarchies, was at its height and the ugly spectre of popular revolution was absent from the feast. There were no serious disturbances to the ordered hierarchic society and the conspicuous consumption of royal and aristocratic families that have left for posterity stunning proofs of their patronage of artists and craftsmen. The 'Sun King', Louis XIV, presided over an effulgently glittering court at Versailles and set the tone for neighbouring monarchs to emulate. You will read of splendid battles fought and won by talented generals like the Duke of Marlborough, who defeated the French at Malplaquet in this very year. You may find reference to the surprising triumph of Peter the Great at the Battle of Poltava. You will learn that, despite the wars, art, science, philosophy, literature and architecture were flourishing in Europe. You will learn how this spectacular and superior European culture was beginning to export itself around the globe and establish mimetic hierarchies in the Americas. You may be directed to the works of the great polymath Gottfried Leibnitz, who, in this same year, was putting the final touches to his *Théodicée*, a magisterial philosophical tome covering most aspects of the human condition, in which he asserted that God had placed his human creatures in the best of all possible worlds.

Whether the majority of eighteenth-century Europeans would have agreed with him may be doubted. Even if we leave aside those areas which were devastated by the armed conflicts of the major powers that raged intermittently for many years, life was never easy for the inhabitants of central Europe. 'Germany', a term of convenience we use to refer to the greater part of this geographical area, simply did not exist. What did exist was a patchwork of some three hundred petty states, within ambiguous and fluctuating borders, each guarding its own customs and privileges, each harbouring its own ambitions, each jealously eyeing the territory of its neighbours. This politically unstable continent could never know meaningful peace as long as it was a prey to great-power rivalries and smal-power inter-state tensions.

All this you may well glean from the standard histories. What you will almost certainly find no reference to is the Great Freeze. And this, despite the fact that it changed Europe more profoundly than all the activities of kings, parliaments and armies put together. It transformed the political balance in the East and North. It gave a new impetus to colonial settlement. It changed the shape of economic activity. It shifted large masses of Europe's population. It created new fashions. And it killed more people than all the wars that had raged for half a century or more. And that puts us human beings in our place. It reminds us that all our endeavours – good and bad – may at any time be swept into the dustbin of history. No one knows what caused the Great Freeze, but the fact is that for a mere three months out of the last half-millennium Europe was subjected to arctic conditions the like of which it had never before experienced and which it has never since experienced. We need to be humble enough to allot the Great Freeze its appropriate place in our story.

Chapter 6

1848

It is usually known as the 'Year of Revolutions' but a more meaningful title might be the 'Year of Confusion' or the 'Year of Blighted Hopes'. There is nothing strange about popular risings against offensive regimes. What is unusual about 1848 is that similar protest movements erupted everywhere. All over Europe people protested, marched, demonstrated or took up arms determined to make their societies fairer, their governments accountable, their national borders secure. Like all revolutionaries in all places and at all times, they were demanding 'justice' and 'liberty'. The end results were tens of thousands slain and aspirations crushed.

The varied discontents that gushed forth like water from a multi-holed barrel had been many years accumulating. A whole generation earlier, in 1815, the ancient monarchies of Europe – Austria, Prussia, Britain, Russia – and their allies had ganged up on the dictator, Napoleon Bonaparte, who had made himself master of the continent, and defeated him at the Battle of Waterloo. The kings and ministers who returned to office after a quarter of a century of war against the French and their emperor blithely assumed they could, at last, put out the 'Business as Usual' signs. Everything could go back to being the way it had been before – the way it was meant to be by God. The Almighty appointed his deputies – popes, kings and emperors – to rule in his name. Beneath them a hierarchy of aristocrats, gentlemen, bishops and bureaucrats exercised authority over populations whose duty it was to obey their betters and not to question the divine ordering of society.

The only trouble with that theory was that the world of post-1815 was *not* the world of pre-1789. When, on 14 July 1789, a Paris mob had stormed the royal prison of the Bastille, thus setting off the French Revolution, they had been driven by resentments and aspirations. In the bloody outcome the king, Louis XVI, and hundreds of royalist supporters had been executed. The new republican government had survived until 1804, when it was abolished by Napoleon, the general it had hired to do its dirty work. In a series of brilliant campaigns he extended the boundaries of the state until his French Empire became the biggest Europe had seen for a thousand years. After his fall the leaders of the victorious monarchies redrew the map, restoring independence to conquered nations and putting the old ruling families back in control. In 1815 Louis XVIII occupied his brother's throne. He and his fellow sovereigns returned to their luxurious palaces.

But the resentments and aspirations that had swept their ilk from power were still very much in evidence. More than that – they were now wide-spread and with deeper roots than before, and they continued to manifest themselves in outbreaks of unrest over the following years. In fact, we should not think of the French Revolution and the Napoleonic Wars as causes of upheaval across Europe. Rather, they were symptoms of a profound disturbance beneath the surface of everyday life and, like slumbering volcanoes, occasionally broke forth in violence and mayhem. Anyone who lived between 1780 and 1848 and who was aware of what was happening in the world beyond his or her own town or village was conscious of an atmosphere of continuous social tension.

There were three main reasons why ordinary folk across Europe were restless. The first was the impact of industrialisation. By concentrating manual workers and semi-skilled artisans in factory towns, technological progress created a self-conscious underclass. The life of the agrarian poor had never been particularly rosy but they had been scattered in small communities under the patronage of aris-tocratic or gentry landowners and they were only rarely able to combine together to seek improvement of their wages or working conditions. But, as families moved into the increasingly overcrowded streets of towns and cities in search of jobs, they discovered a new solidarity and were susceptible to the fiery oratory of rabble-rousers. The political class, made up of landowners and nouveau-riche industrialists, were determined to maintain the status quo and regarded with ill-concealed hostility any attempt by the workers to demand a say in the way they were treated and governed. To the masters such activity smacked of treason and was certainly against the law of nature. 'We are encouraged to fling the boroughs into the hands of a poor, ignorant and venal proletariat' – so one letter writer to the London *Times* responded to the suggestion that some members of the labouring class might be allowed to vote. This was why most countries had anti-combination laws – laws forbidding public gatherings of two or more people – and maintained censorship of the press. Europe was like a pressure cooker; a head of steam was building up inside, while those in power were keeping the lid clamped firmly down.

The second impetus for reform came from the rise of liberalism. European society was not divided simply between oppressed workers and reactionary masters. There existed a significant minority of social and political idealists. Comprising largely students, lawyers, professional men and upper-class philanthropists, the liberal movement favoured change by constitutional means. Liberals did not condone revolution. Rather, they insisted that the only way to avoid it was by extending the franchise in order to create parliaments capable of ridding the existing system of its injustices.

The third component of discontent was nationalism. People have always striven to know who they are, to be clear about what distinguishes them from other people. And any attempt to define what was meant by, for example, 'Poland', 'Italy' or 'Germany' involved considerations of ethnicity, religion and cultural tradition. We have seen in recent years how the struggle for identity has led to appalling violence in the Balkans and parts of Africa. In the early nineteenth century Europe was riven by similar disputes. Two kinds of nationalism were in conflict. One was the 'top-down' type, imposed by statesmen who believed that by defining frontiers they could make the people living within those frontiers adopt a shared identity, irrespective of their own origins. It was, after all, happening in the USA; British, German, Italian, Russian, Dutch and other immigrants were forging a new nation. What was sauce for the New World goose would, surely, serve just as well for the Old World gander. But America was a new country peopled by immigrants who wanted to make a new start. In Europe cultural roots ran deep and were firmly attached to the soil. The Holy Roman Empire had embraced Austrians, Hungarians, Germans, Italians, Czechs, Slovenes and Poles. Napoleon had abolished that empire, only to establish his rule over a still more diverse collection of nationalities. When the victorious nations met at the Congress of Vienna (1814) they gave some recognition to the claims of small countries to self-determination, but they were largely preoccupied with dividing up the territorial spoils among themselves and hemming France in with 'buffer states' to prevent any repeat of its expansionism. Thus, for example, Holland, Belgium and Luxembourg were lumped together as one state, while Piedmont in North Italy and the island of Sardinia became a united kingdom. Austria still controlled parts of North Italy. Russia lorded it over Poles and Finns.

But there was another kind of nationalism – 'bottom-up' nationalism – and its roots were deep. It was fed by poets, musicians, painters and historians who were conscious of the power residing in old legends, traditional songs and the very landscape beloved by families who had lived within it for generations. The Brothers Grimm collected German folk tales. Frederick Chopin, from his exile in France, turned traditional Polish dance tunes into passionate expressions of national identity. Richard Wagner turned medieval German legends into elaborate operas. The French painter, Eugène Delacroix, looked for inspiration to stirring incidents in his country's history. The composer Bedrich Smetana expressed the landscape of his beloved Bohemia in orchestral music. History and culture could not be suppressed. One way and another, the overthrow of the French superstate had left an enormous amount of unfinished business.

Much of it remained to be tackled thirty-three years later. During those thirty-three years there were sporadic conflagrations as subject peoples and downtrodden classes struggled for freedom, only to be met by determined and inhuman shows of force. In 1831 a revolt of the Poles was put down with utter ruthlessness by Russia. Afterwards 80,000 'traitors against the tsar' who had not been shot or hanged were exiled to Siberia. It was a distance of some 6,500 kilometres and they – men, women and children – were obliged to walk, roped together or loaded with chains. Thousands, of course, did not survive the ordeal.

Violent repression, inevitably, provoked violent reaction. Intransigence pushed potential rebels into political extremism. Several leaders of social or nationalistic reform were driven into exile, from where they planned revolt or published their theories of political change. Two such radical thinkers were Karl Marx and Friedrich Engels, members of a German underground group meeting in Paris, called the League of the Just, a moderate socialist combination. By 1847 they had taken refuge in London and it was there that, the following February, they had printed the *Communist Manifesto*. This treatise on social and economic theory did not fuel the revolutions of 1848; but it did seem to reflect the resentment many protesters were feeling and it appeared to give logical authentication to their yearnings for a radically different society. Marx and Engels insisted that, despite all outward appearances, the monied classes were not the inevitable leaders of the world. History was on the side of the workers – the proletariat – who were poised to wrest control from the hands of their oppressors. As they said, 'What the bourgeoisie produces is its own gravediggers.' They dismissed the flabby democratic ideals of the liberals, insisting that democracy was only a smiling mask covering the ugly features of capitalist domination.

By the time the *Communist Manifesto* came off the presses, revolution was well under way and spreading fast. Italy, a country divided into six separate states, was the first to burst into insurrection. On 12 February radicals in the Sicilian city of Palermo went onto the streets in protest against misrule by King Ferdinand II, who ruled both the island and the mainland territory of Naples. The rebels gained what seemed initially to be a complete victory. Ferdinand buckled and granted Sicily its own constitution. This easy success emboldened other would-be revolutionaries. There was no coherence to the demands of the radicals. Some wanted liberal constitutions. Others called for the complete abolition of hereditary monarchy and the setting-up of popular republics. And there were those who argued that the peninsula would never be able to shake off Austrian control and the interference of other reactionary regimes until all its people came together to forge a united Italy. The rulers of the several states were quick to follow Ferdinand's example and grant a degree of representative government. Some acted from liberal sentiment. Some hoped by modest concessions to stave off full-blown insurrection. Others were simply playing for time, believing that the revolution would eventually run out of steam.

The exception to this general rule was the Austrian-ruled states of sub-Alpine North Italy, Lombardy and Venetia. In January the citizens of Milan, the Lombard capital, united in what might seem to have been a mild protest – they refused to buy lottery tickets or tobacco. But these commodities carried heavy taxes, and the recalcitrance of their Italian subjects so enraged the authorities that a tense situation rapidly developed, as a result of which Austrian soldiers killed sixty-one Lombards for 'inciting rebellion'. Making martyrs is always a mistake; it is a sign of frustration and failure and it usually encourages as many people as it deters. The bloody reaction of the Austrians provoked further demonstrations, which led to the Milanese rising up en masse and driving out the Austrian troops in March.

But by then the Italian revolutionaries knew that they were not alone. All over Europe people were rising up against their masters. We can only understand the rapid development of widespread violence by examining what was happening simultaneously in various countries.

In France an uprising in 1830 had swept away the reactionary regime of King Charles X and replaced it with the liberal monarchy of King Louis-Philippe. The new government believed that moderate reforms such as the abolition of censorship would satisfy the masses, but left-wing activists rejected the paternalistic attitude of the king and his ministers and claimed *as of right* further changes, such as the extension of the franchise. Only substantial land-holders, about one per cent of the population, were allowed to vote. When bad harvests and economic recession hit the country in 1846–7, agitators found a ready audience among the poor and unemployed. Because political meetings were forbidden, liberals and socialists got round the regulations by holding 'banquets', celebratory meals at which radical ideas were discussed and propaganda distributed. One such, planned for 14 January, was banned by the government. It was rescheduled for 22 February, then, at the last moment, cancelled. Paris was immediately in uproar. Louis-Philippe, looking for a scapegoat, sacked his unpopular chief minister, François Guizot. This news drew an excited crowd to the Foreign Affairs office, which was swiftly protected by a cordon of troops. We are familiar with such scenes and know how difficult it is for police to contain angry crowds. Nineteenth-century French National Guardsmen were not issued with riot shields. Their only means of protection was the deterrent influence of their muskets and bayonets. The officers tried to control their men and instil calm but it only took one nervous soldier's trigger finger to tighten involuntarily for a volley of shots to be fired. Fifty-two people lay sprawled in their own blood on the cobbles. It was a declaration of war.

Angry citizens took possession of their capital by the characteristically French expedient of building barricades. Carts, wagons, omnibuses and furniture were piled up to keep government forces at bay. But many members of the National Guard refused to fire upon their own people. The military arsenal was raided and the mob became an armed mob. Within hours total confusion reigned in the city. On 24 February a panic-stricken Louis-Philippe abdicated and fled, doubtless calling to mind the guillotining of his predecessor in 1793. In the National Assembly, liberal politician Alexis de Tocqueville deplored the blindness of the nation's leaders. 'Look at what is happening within the working classes,' he thundered. 'Can you not see that ideas are gradually spreading among them which are not only going to overthrow certain laws, but society itself, knocking it off the foundations on which it rests today?' Opposition politicians cobbled together a republican constitution and declared that elections would be held on the basis of adult male suffrage. In less than a week a comparatively bloodless coup had swept away the old order, seemingly for good.

Matters were more complicated in Germany because Germany itself was more complicated. It was a confederacy of thirty-nine principalities. Many of them were incorporated in the Austro-Hungarian Empire, ruled from Vienna, while the emperor directly ruled Hungary. In northern Germany the dominant power was Prussia. Throughout these lands, radicals were demanding democratic assemblies and press freedom. There was also a deep nationalistic yearning for German identity and solidarity. In Austria the chief minister and patron of autocratic regimes was Prince Klemens von Metternich. He had, for many years, dominated German politics and European diplomacy and, though his power was much diminished by 1848, he was still the hated symbol of repression. When sparks from Paris ignited the resentments of Austrian liberals, Metternich became the focus of angry demonstrations. More potentially disastrous for the empire was the news that the freedom epidemic had spread to Hungary, which geographically made up the greater part of the Austrian state. On 13 March Metternich was forced to resign. His was an important scalp. The feeble-minded Emperor Ferdinand summoned the National Diet (parliament) and agreed to allow the discussion of a new constitution. Next day the threatened rising in Hungary took place. Peasants congregating in Buda-Pest for an annual fair were stirred up by popular orators to storm public buildings. Here, too, Ferdinand hastened to concede fresh elections to a more representative assembly.

In Prussia King Frederick William IV also tried to stave off criticism by introducing reforms. He promised to allow a constitutional debate, to grant press freedom and to support the pan-German programme. Unfortunately, his past record did not encourage optimism. In times of crisis he had made concessions, only to cancel them once the danger had passed. On 18 March the Berlin mob copied the militant protest of the Parisians. They threw up barricades and defied the royal troops. The result was the same as in the French capital – only worse. This time the dead were numbered in hundreds. Frederick William, cynically following the principle that ends justify means, publicly ate a large slice of humble pie. He made a great show of supporting liberal and nationalist demands, promised constitutional reform and on 21 March led a procession through the streets of Berlin to the cemetery where the 'martyrs' of the uprising had been buried, wearing the black, red and gold tricolour, symbol of a united Germany.

This was the same day that news arrived in Berlin of another serious defeat for autocratic monarchy. Ludwig I of Bavaria was an aesthete king, with a passion for art and women. His long-running affair with the Irish-born actress, Lola Montez, scandalised many of his subjects and there was resentment at the high taxes levied to support ambitious building projects and foreign policies. Ludwig, for all his faults, had the courage of his convictions. When the reform movement reached Munich and his own cabinet urged him to make concessions, he insisted that it would be a betrayal of his sacred position as monarch to be dictated to by his subjects. Rather than suffer such a humiliation, on 20 March he abdicated in favour of his eldest son, Maximilian, whom he thoroughly detested.

Over the centuries, whatever game Europe's nations played, the weakest hand always seemed to be dealt to Poland. Situated in that part of the continent where the interests of more-powerful neighbours met, the land of the Poles was a permanent buffer, to be divided up, occupied and maintained in the interests of other peoples rather than its own.

Some Polish historians have referred to their land as the 'plaything of the gods', and that is a very apt metaphor. The remarkable fact is that the fierce sense of Polish nationhood could never be crushed. On the contrary, the country's leaders persistently took advantage of every major shift in European affairs to bid for independence. One Polish poet expressed his undying optimism thus:

> Hail, O Christ, Thou Lord of Men!
> Poland in thy footsteps treading
> Like thee suffers, at thy bidding
> Like Thee, too, shall rise again.

Many Poles, in 1848, were under Austrian or Prussian rule, but the greater part of their land had been incorporated into Russia. The people were suffering appallingly. Polish universities were closed and students obliged to study in St Petersburg, where they could be effectively brainwashed. As well as the activists deported to Siberia, over 6,000 had become voluntary exiles, most of them living in France, from where they plotted and schemed for the liberation of their country. Nationalists hoped that, as part of the movement towards self-determination that was blossoming in several parts of the continent, they would be helped to throw off the shackles of Russian domination. They naturally looked to Prussia for help, hoping that a combination of the new liberal government and big-power rivalry would provide them with the necessary military backing.

For a while it seemed that their hopes were well founded. Public speeches in Berlin proclaimed commitment to a united Germany and a free Poland. Writing in the *Neue Rheinische Zeitung*, Marx and Engels declared that freeing Poland was the first priority of the international proletariat. Several exiles congregated in Berlin to consolidate plans with the new government and, in Poznan, capital of Prussian Poland, demonstrations on 20 March resulted in the sending of a delegation to Berlin. But from the beginning rival nationalisms undermined Polish ambitions. Freeing Poland from Russia might well lead, the Berlin parliament realised, to demands for freedom from Prussia. On 23 March Frederick William received a Polish delegation and assured them of his support, but he also issued instructions that any uprising in Prussian-controlled Poland was to be firmly suppressed. He had no desire to see the balance of power upset by redrawing the boundaries yet again. Race-related incidents did not help the Polish cause. Complaining to the Poznan assembly of attacks on their property, Prussian delegates warned: 'Through such acts of infamous violence you stain the honour of your nation and undermine the sympathy for your cause among the nations of Germany and Europe.'

But ethnic clashes multiplied and, on 3 April, the Poznan government rejected the inclusion of their land in a new German empire.

Plans were now well advanced for the creation of this novel pan-German entity. In almost every German state there had been liberal demonstrations, some peaceful, some violent. It was not difficult to attract popular leaders to a convention that would lead Germany into a new, bright, united future. On 31 March a group of politicians met in St Paul's Church, Frankfurt, to organise elections to the first German parliament. They acted with commendable haste and, on 18 May, the new assembly convened in Frankfurt. The time had come to turn fine oratory and radical zeal into political reality.

By now revolution in Italy had become war. All of North Italy from the Po valley to the Alps was inflamed with the desire for freedom from Austria, and the conflagration had spread still farther. There were risings in Trieste and all along the Dalmatian coast. It was obvious that the imperial government could not sit back and watch the dismemberment of its territory. The Milanese rebels looked for help to face the Austrian backlash. They made an alliance with Charles Albert, the moderate king of neighbouring Piedmont-Sardinia. On 24 March he despatched an army across the border into Lombardy to confront the forces of the veteran (he was eighty-two) general and national hero Josef Radetzky. The Austrian commander withdrew his men into strong mountain fortresses, leaving his adversary to take the initiative. This was the crucial moment for the Italian revolt. Charles Albert sent to Florence, Rome, Venice and Naples for other states to join him but, instead of pressing home his advantage and giving the lead which would have inspired his potential allies, he hesitated. Radetzky received reinforcements and went onto the offensive. The other Italian states (except Venice) got cold feet and Piedmont-Sardinia found itself alone against the might of the Austro-Hungarian Empire. Even though chaos reigned in Vienna, the emperor's army was more than a match for Charles Albert's inexperienced and poorly led troops. Radetzky joked that his men should be careful not to kill any of Charles Albert's officers because they were on his side. But what he underestimated was the courage of his enemy. The Italians fought doggedly throughout the summer and the final battle was a bloody one. It was waged at Custoza, near Verona, and lasted two days. In the violent hand-to-hand fighting, half the combatants on both sides were killed. Tens of thousands of Lombard refugees now fled into Piedmont with the retreating army while Radetzky seized Milan. But the effort had drained his men and he was happy to agree a truce with Charles Albert. The conflict between the old order and the new in Italy was not over.

Meanwhile, in France the situation degenerated into confusion and violence. The new assembly was having to deal with what de Tocqueville had warned them about – the clamorous demands of the socialists. The provisional government set up in February was a loose alliance of several factions. Some wanted a limited monarchy; others an out-and-out republic. Some believed effective power should remain safely in middle-class hands; others demanded universal manhood suffrage. Now that they had taken power away from the Crown, they had to make good their claim to speak for the people. This they could not do with any conviction. The assembly was not Paris and Paris was not France. The reformers gathered in the Hôtel de Ville were very conscious of the socialist mobs and their fiery orators who controlled the streets. Their daily postbag was stuffed with demands for a host of social and economic reforms that no government could have delivered in the short term. And beyond the excitements of the capital lay a rural France in which communities were still controlled by local landlords and the clergy, a conservative France that viewed with suspicion the clamorous demagogues of the metropolis.

They did their best. They cobbled together a hasty programme of reform, including provision of poor relief, legislation restricting working hours and abolition of press censorship. They fixed a general election for 23 April and decreed that all Frenchmen over twenty-one would have the vote. At one stroke the electorate was extended from 200,000 to 9,000,000, most of whom were illiterate, had not been prepared for political responsibility and were influenced by the leaders of local society. As a result the election returned only a hundred or so radicals and socialists. The remaining 770 seats were divided between monarchists and moderate liberals. It was a shock for the extremists to discover that they did not speak for the majority of the people. They refused to accept their rejection, claiming, as defeated parties so often do, that the election had been rigged. The new parliament had been sitting for only three days when, on 15 May, a mob broke in upon it and declared it dissolved. The socialists set up a rival assembly. The legitimate government had no alternative but to call in the National Guard. More blood was spilled. Socialist leaders were imprisoned or fled into exile. Their organisations were banned. Resentment simmered in the stifling summer streets. In mid-June the barricades went up again. Armed demonstrators fought pitched battles with government troops who only prevailed by training cannon on the barricades. As the soldiers regained possession of Paris street by street, they massacred their fellow citizens mercilessly. The aftermath saw the jails bulging with 11,000 prisoners, several of whom were summarily executed. Thus, liberal reformers found themselves using the methods of the old regime they so much deplored and for the same reason – to stay in power.

Three days after the May riots in Paris, the much-heralded pan-German parliament had convened in Frankfurt. It represented the complete spectrum of political opinion. Its 586 members divided almost equally between right-wing, centrist and left-wing parties. More importantly, the assembly was made up almost entirely of theorists with no prior political experience. University professors, school teachers, lawyers and other professionals were well equipped to debate the relative merits of monarchy and republicanism, the acceptability of Austria-Hungary within a German confedera-tion and the degree of autonomy to be granted to regional assemblies. But this talking shop became steadily divorced from reality. On the streets and in the villages, rapidly moving events would make the Frankfurt parliament an irrelevance. Its nose was spectacularly rubbed in the dirt the following April. Members solemnly offered the crown of united Germany to Frederick William IV of Prussia. He turned it down with the comment that he had no interest in 'a bauble that stank of the gutter' and was 'baked in dirt and mud'.

By bending like the willow before the liberal wind of March, the Prussian king was able to emerge as a monarchist oak once that wind had subsided. In the spring of 1848 he retired from the Berlin scene to his palace at Potsdam and surrounded himself with a reactionary clique drawn from the Prussian aristocracy. His ministers countered several of the more-extreme proposals of the assembly. For much of the summer he was preoccupied with a territorial war against Denmark, which, like most wars, had the domestic advantage of whipping up nationalistic feeling. By the autumn a truce had been declared and Frederick William was able to turn all his attention to internal politics. Throughout Europe the democratic experiment was faltering as vested interests reacted against socialism and regional self-determination. In November Frederick William made his well-prepared move to restore full monarchical power. He appointed Count Brandenburg as his chief minister, with instructions to remove the parliament from Berlin to a location where it could be more easily managed. The deputies refused to move and called on the citizenry to support them by refusing to pay their taxes. But the popular mood had changed and there was no new uprising when royal troops turned the deputies out of their chamber. On 5 December the king played his trump card. He declared a new constitution, basically liberal but with retained royal powers. With fresh elections promised, the assembly instituted on 22 May 1848 simply ceased to exist.

The pattern was similar in Austria-Hungary. The emperor had withdrawn to one of his rural palaces, leaving Vienna in the hands of the people's parliament. Ferdinand and his advisers could only play a waiting game and hold their forces in readiness to use as soon as it was safe to do so. Their instinct was to fall back on a strategy that had served the heterogeneous empire well in the past – 'divide and rule'. As long as they could foment discord between Germans and Czechs, Hungarians and Croatians, Poles and Germans, they could prevent the nationalities sinking their differences in common action. But now there was trouble in so many parts of the sprawling empire that old techniques were not guaranteed to work. By the autumn of 1848 Piedmont had been neutralised but Venice was still defying the emperor and its resistance encouraged reformers in other Italian states. The volatility of the situation was demonstrated in the Papal States on 15 November, when the pope's prime minister was knifed by an assassin and Pius IX fled for safety to the kingdom of Naples. In Rome a republic was proclaimed and a liberal government instituted a reforming programme.

In Hungary the reformed assembly led by the nationalist hero, Lajos Kossuth, had established a large measure of autonomy, but the weak chink in its armour was the domination of ethnic minorities by the Magyar majority. In September the Austrian government despatched an army to Buda-Pest, led by the Croatian general – and sworn enemy of the Magyars – Josip Jelačić. The Hungarian capital fell quite quickly but that did not end the war. The government decamped to Debrecen, where it formally deposed the emperor and proclaimed Hungary an independent republic. In Vienna the imperial regime had now re-established control and a new emperor, Franz Josef, was taking a tougher line. Even so, the Austrians were unable to crush the rebels single-handedly. They had to call on Tsar Nicholas I for aid and it was a Russian army that finally defeated the Hungarians the following August. Again, the cost of failure was appalling. Thousands died in battle, hundreds were executed, yet more exiles were forced to leave their homeland. To demonstrate their contempt for the Hungarians, Nicholas's generals even ordered prominent women to be publicly flogged. Hungary was then divided into new administrative units and subjected to far tighter control than it had experienced before. And minority races who had helped to bring down the Magyars gained nothing for their loyalty to the emperor. One Croat ruefully remarked: 'What the Magyars received as punishment, we had as our reward.'

The movement for Italian unification now attracted the talents of two remarkable men, Giuseppe Mazzini and Giuseppi Garibaldi. These committed revolutionaries were the Castro and

Guevara of their day, fiercely patriotic men who were clear about their revolutionary principles and were prepared to fight for them. Like their twenti-eth-century counterparts, they had been involved in earlier political struggles, for which they had suffered imprisonment and exile. In February 1849 they came together in Rome, Mazzini as the leader of a republican government pledged to the unifica-tion of Italy and Garibaldi as the military supremo, commanding his dedicated 'Red Shirts', experts in guerrilla warfare.

By this time the hopes of liberals, socialists, democrats and nationalists were beginning to run into the sand. All along, the disparate movements had been strong on idealism and weak on organisa-tion. They had been too divided in their respective aims and ambitions to combine effectively against the autocratic regimes they strove to replace. It was only a matter of time before all the flickering hopes were snuffed. If we can discern any single moment when the doom of liberal democracy was sealed, one contender would be 10 December 1848. That was the date of the first presidential election in the French republic. The name of the successful candi-date was Bonaparte! Not the long-dead emperor, but Louis Napoleon Bonaparte, his nephew. This son of a family still revered by many in France had lived several years in exile across the English Channel. This contributed considerably to his success in the election. He was not tarred with the brush of political discord and failure like his opponents. What he offered and what the reputation of his uncle seemed to support was strong government, an end to the chaos of party strife and a zero tolerance attitude towards socialist extremism. Two years later he would seize dictatorial power and proclaim himself emperor.

It was Louis Napoleon, the leader of republican France, who crushed the republican movement in Italy. His own position depended on his ability to balance political forces in the national assembly, where conservative elements were growing in strength. To win the approval of the right wing and of Catholics throughout France, he set out on a crusade to rescue the pope. In April 1849 he sent an army composed of contingents from France, Austria, Spain and Naples, under French leadership, to lay siege to Rome. The first round in the war went to Garibaldi, but the sheer numerical strength of the enemy meant they could cut Rome off from all potential supporters and, by the beginning of July, the city had been starved into submission. The King of Piedmont had already suffered a similar defeat. Renewing Piedmontese defiance of Austria, he had led his army to a crushing defeat at Novara in March. It was now Venice's turn to suffer siege. After a remorseless bombardment by Austrian artillery, the 'queen of the Adriatic' surrendered on

22 August. That was the last episode in the saga of Italian democracy and independence.

As to the great German parliament, it simply disintegrated. Austria and Prussia both withdrew their delegates as soon as their own internal disorders had been dealt with. In June 1849 a rump assembly reconvened in Stuttgart, capital of the kingdom of Württemberg, only to be dispersed by troops sent by the king.

As the autocrats of Europe regained their thrones and consolidated their power, another, greater monarch made his rule known to devastating effect. As if the disillusionment experienced by idealists and the sufferings inflicted on those who had dared to strive for political freedom and national identity were not enough, this merciless king led his cohorts across the continent from the summer of 1848 and compounded their misery. His name was Cholera. A deadly epidemic, originating in Asia, spread inexorably westwards. It was particularly virulent in the towns and cities, where people lived in close communities, which aided contagion. These were the very places where liberal assemblies met and where radical mobs gathered. Historians concerned to unravel the political and social complexities of the 'Year of Revolutions' can easily overlook the debilitating effects of disease. Cholera killed hundreds of thousands, including active campaigners for reform who, until they were struck down, had stirred and inspired the masses. Those who escaped death were left chronically weakened, with little energy to continue fighting for their cause. As one historian has said, 1848 was a year 'bounded by calamity, and the embers that had been partly kindled by hunger were partly quenched by disease'.

After 1848 there were more autocrats in Europe than there had been before. Thousands of men, women and children lay in freshly-dug graves. Thousands languished in fetid, overcrowded prisons. And still more thousands lived in exile, driven from home and family by their stubborn adherence to a set of ideals. Constitutions which had given people some say in how they were governed had been, for the most part, rescinded. No part of the continent had been unaffected by the political changes that had taken place or the disillusionment that had followed. Idealists who had earnestly campaigned for rulers to give 'power to the people' had lost their nerve when they discovered that the people might actually take that power for themselves. Middle-class urban liberals, no less than wealthy landowners on their country estates, were terrified by the spectre of what Marx and Engels called the 'dictatorship of the proletariat'. Only in Switzerland did revolution lead to permanent change. A brief civil war was won by the advocates of liberal reform. They established a federal republic and a constitution that granted many civic freedoms, guaranteed by a legislature modelled on the United States Congress.

So what had it all been about? Had anything been achieved apart from widespread misery? Do the events of 1848 indicate the impotence – perhaps even the folly – of grand principles? Is political man no different from the brute beasts, of whom Wordsworth observed:

> ... the good old rule
> Sufficeth them, the ancient plan,
> That they should take who have the power
> And they should keep who can.

The year of revolutions revealed a humanity red in tooth and claw. Politics is, as Otto von Bismarck remarked, 'the art of the possible'. Bismarck was the great Prussian statesman of the next generation, the man who *did* succeed in creating a united Germany. His verdict on idealism was harsh: 'Not by speeches and votes of the majority are the great questions of the time decided – that was the error of 1848–9 – but by iron and blood.' We may call that cynicism or realism. What matters is that Bismarck's is not the only voice. Among the more sensitive souls and creative minds of the mid-nineteenth century were people who did believe in principles worth fighting and dying for. They were not all orators. Wagner and Chopin both experienced exile. Honoré Daumier applied his brush to revealing the appalling conditions in which the poor existed. Charles Dickens similarly exposed exploitation and injustice. Eugène Delacroix expressed the revolution in paint and Giuseppe Verdi's operas explored the agonies of downtrodden people. The polymath, Victor Hugo, combined poetry and novel writing with ardent journalism and membership of the French National Assembly. They were among the many who could not disassociate themselves from the sufferings and aspirations, hopes and fears, triumphs and miseries of their contemporaries. Self-interest and sheer bestiality have shaped much of human history. But they have not been the only forces at work.

Chapter 7

1865–6

Deep rents in the fabric of society take generations, even centuries to mend. If winning a peace is more difficult than winning a war, winning an internal peace in a divided country is many times harder. This is basically why the immediate aftermath of the American Civil War (1861–65) was so immensely tragic. What was called the time of 'Reconstruction' was no such thing. No lasting settlement could be built upon the unstable foundation of the ideological differences that persisted between the 'free' northern and 'slave-owning' southern states of the USA. There were widely disparate expectations about the position of freed Negroes in post war America. There was deep mistrust between those who gathered from the two sides to negotiate a new settlement. This mistrust gave rise to unco-operativeness, repeated violent confrontations and a constitutional conflict that very nearly tore the nation apart.

'I can embody it all in a few words: beggary, starvation, death, bitter grief, utter want of hope.' That was the verdict on these months of Henry Timrod, the 'laureate of the Confederacy'. The poet could speak for thousands of men and women from the southern states of the USA because he shared their experiences to the full. In the civil war, which had just ended, his business had been ruined and he and his wife had had to sell up everything in order to buy food. The coming of peace after years of war is usually a time of rejoicing or at least of relief. This was not the case in the aftermath of the conflict that had tragically divided the slave-owning Confederate states of America from the free societies of the Unionist North. Around 620,000 combatant troops had died in battle. An incalculable multitude of other men and women had fallen victim to starvation or disease. The economy of a large part of the country had been shattered. Farms, villages and towns were reduced to mounds of cold ash. More importantly, bitter hatreds had been sown which would, for many generations, go on producing an evil crop.

By 1861 mainland USA stretched from coast to coast and had almost assumed its present shape. Its constituent parts were either full states of the Union or associated territories. But, at the same time, a stark line of division ran between the members of the nation. Slavery, which had been a major moral issue throughout the Western world since the beginnings of the campaign against the slave trade in the 1770s, was the problem. The southern American states from Virginia to Texas relied largely on plantation agriculture. Producing the cash crops of cotton and tobacco was highly profitable but it was also labour-intensive. It needed a large, cheap workforce. Before abolition, slaves had been imported from Africa. These and their descendants constituted an underclass numbering three and a half million by the mid-nineteenth century. The North, by contrast, was a society of small farms and industrial towns. Its state legislatures had abolished slavery. As the Union expanded and new states were admitted, the dominant issue was whether each fresh member would be a slave-owning state or a free state. The southerners saw themselves being steadily outnumbered and subject to a mounting demand for abolition. They firmly resisted what they saw as a challenge, not only to their economic viability, but also to their entire way of life and the racial philosophy that sustained it. In February 1861 six southern states seceded from the Union and, by the end of the year, they had been joined by five others. These Confederate states established their own government with its headquarters at Richmond, Virginia, levied their own taxes and issued their own currency. They took over federal offices, garrisons, dockyards and arsenals and made it clear that they would deploy their resources against any attempt at coercion.

The government in Washington, led by President Abraham Lincoln, could only regard this defiance as treason and sent reinforcements to threatened Union positions. When, on 12 April 1861, Confederate forces opened fire on the garrison at Fort Sumter, Charleston, South Carolina, the American Civil War had begun. Almost exactly four years later, on 9 April 1865, the main Confederate army, led by General Robert E. Lee, surrendered to the Union commander-in-chief, General Ulysses S. Grant. The rival military leaders treated their adversaries with courtesy and the soldiers began, slowly, to make their way homewards. But if anyone thought that the reunited nation could put behind it the bitterness of the war, they were soon horrifically disillusioned. Five days after the surrender President Lincoln was shot by a fanatical secessionist assassin as he watched a play at Ford's Theatre, Washington. The murderer, John Wilkes Booth, a dyed-in-the-wool racist and member of the Confederate intelligence service, tricked his way into the presidential box and, screaming (according to an eyewitness) 'Revenge for the South', shot Lincoln at point-blank range. Whatever the military outcome of the conflict, hatred remained lodged in many hearts.

National recovery was now the government's priority. The cost of the war in terms of human misery and suffering was incalculable, but there were bills to be paid and they could be reckoned. The cost of the war to the federal and state treasuries was a staggering $20 billion, a debt that would take half a century to eradicate. With the benefit of the long view it is obvious that recovery could take place only if national money and resources were channelled into restoring the economy and society of the worst affected areas. Certainly, inspectors sent from Washington were in no doubt about the size of the problem. One of them described war-torn Charleston in these words:

A city... of vacant houses, of widowed women, of rotting wharves, of deserted warehouses, of weed-wild gardens, of miles of grass-grown streets, of acres of pitiful and voiceless barrenness...

Richmond, Virginia, capital of the Confederacy, was 'in ruins, as far as the eye could reach... Beds of cinders, cellars half filled with bricks and rubbish, broken and blackened walls, impassable streets deluged with debris'. Conditions were no better in the countryside: 'The fences were all gone... the barns were all burned; chimneys standing without houses and houses standing without roofs or doors or windows... bridges all destroyed, roads badly cut up.' Banks were closed. Southern currency and state bonds were valueless. Shop shelves were empty. Farmland could not rapidly be brought back into production. Businesses (many of them tied to the agricultural economy) were bankrupt. Roads, bridges and rail tracks were devastated. The crisis inevitably brought out the worst in many Americans. Desperate need and sheer opportunism drove people to crime. People engaged in looting, burglary and demanding money with menaces and claimed 'necessity' as justification for their actions. Police and law courts were either inoperative or ineffective. Over large areas civilised society simply ceased to exist.

What cruelly pointed up the plight of the South was the contrast with life in the North. There, galloping economic progress was being made. The 1860s was a decade of remarkable expansion. Immigrants were arriving in ever-growing numbers, to seek work in the eastern states or to try their luck in the prairie lands to the west. As frontiersmen pushed the national boundary steadily eastwards, fencing off farmland and founding new towns, manufacturers enjoyed a boom, supplying the settlers with the necessities of everyday life. Factory building increased by 80% during the decade. Railroad barons flung iron tracks across the continent. Telegraph companies provided the nation with an up-to-date communications infrastructure. The discovery of oil gave rise to another new industry. The world's first mercantile multimillionaires appeared and names like Rockefeller and Vanderbilt symbolised what the American dream was all about. Some of their capitalist friends had made their fortunes in ways directly connected with the conflict. War is always a profitable business for those ready to take advantage of it; someone has to make the uniforms and military transports and ammunition and guns. United action, coordinated from the centre but involving all interested parties, was the only way the devastated region could be got back on its feet. But there was no way that all interested parties could be induced to sing from the same sheet. The difference in ethos between the thrusting, individualistic North and the aristocratic, paternalistic South could not have been greater. It was this difference that undermined the Reconstruction.

Politicians at federal and state level had a threefold problem to solve. It was layered, like the rings of an onion. Its outer skin presented the obvious urgency of getting the southern economy back on its feet. Towns, plantations, railways and government buildings had to be cleared from the wreckage of war and restored to working order. People had to be provided with jobs to do and houses to live in. That would need capital investment and that begged the question of how the money was to be raised. Could a broken society be taxed to meet the costs of the crisis it had itself precipitated? If extra funding was needed from the North, what strings might be attached to it? Would northern capitalists be encouraged to help with the recovery and, if so, would they be regarded as money-grubbing interlopers making profit out of the misery of the South?

The second layer was political. How were the secessionist states to be readmitted to the Union? On what terms? At what cost in adjusting their own laws, customs and social conventions?

From that it follows that the third and deepest layer was what has been called 'inner reconstruction'. Assuming that prosperity could be restored and the political mechanisms put in place to maintain it, could ingrained attitudes – and particularly those relating to race – be changed? At a stroke all black slaves had been freed. What would happen to this jobless multitude? Could southern whites be persuaded to live as equals alongside their former slaves? Could southern blacks be prevented from reacting violently against their erstwhile owners?

The two constitutional issues that faced the post-war USA were the terms on which rebel states were to be readmitted to the Union and who would set those terms – the president or the federal Congress (the bi-cameral parliament of the USA). Lincoln had been clear about the answers to these questions. Before the end of hostilities he had taken presidential initiatives. He had offered amnesties to all southerners who would take an oath of loyalty. He had guaranteed to return to them all their confiscated lands. He had promised to give full recognition to state governments if they renounced slavery and induced a mere ten per cent of their people to take the new oath. But he did not have a united party behind him. His irenic policy was backed by the Democrats, who felt considerable sympathy for the leaders of the southern states, but Lincoln's own party, the Republicans, was divided between moderates and radicals and it was the radicals who were in the majority. Many members of Congress had suffered in the recent conflict. Some had lost sons or brothers in the fighting. They were bent on revenge or, at the very least, on ensuring that the plantation nobility should acknowledge and pay for their crimes. They were not prepared to see the southern leaders return to their bad old ways as though nothing had happened. Whether Lincoln, had he lived, would have been able to carry his policy is open to doubt. What is certain is that the man who replaced him, Andrew Johnson, lacked Lincoln's charisma. He was a southerner, from Tennessee, but refused to join his seceding colleagues. When Tennessee was taken under federal control, Johnson was appointed governor and, in the hope of attracting support from southern Unionists, Lincoln chose him as his running mate in the 1864 election. When he was thrust, unexpectedly, into the presidency and tried to continue his predecessor's policy of reconciliation, Johnson inevitably found himself mistrusted for being too soft on his southern friends. Not a single Confederate leader was tried for treason or war crimes and only one southern officer was executed. Meanwhile, congressmen were inflamed by reports sent to Washington by their agents in the South. 'The number of murders and assaults perpetrated on Negroes is very great,' one of them stated in December,

> As to my personal experience, I will only mention that during my two days' sojourn at Atlanta, one Negro was stabbed with fatal effect on the street and three were poisoned, one of whom died. While I was at Montgomery, one Negro was cut across the throat, and another was shot but both escaped with their lives... It is a sad fact that the perpetration of those acts is not confined to that class of people which might be called the rabble.

Another report spoke of organised gangs in Alabama,

> Who board some of the [river] boats... to hang, shoot or drown the victims they may find on them... the bewildered and terrified freedmen know not what to do – to leave is death; to remain is to suffer

the increased burden imposed on them by the cruel taskmaster…

By the autumn of 1865 the president and the congressional majority were at war with each other. As soon as Congress reconvened in December 1865, it firmly opposed the president's 'appeasement' of the rebels. Members refused to ratify the presidential restitution of ex-Confederate states and did not allow members rehabilitated by the president to take their seats. Strident radicals persisted in regarding the Confederate lands as conquered territories and a joint committee of both houses (the Senate and the House of Representatives) was set up to manage their affairs. Johnson refused to let himself be bullied. He believed (with some justification) that his congressional opponents were acting unconstitutionally. 'Southerners cannot be treated as subjugated people or vassal colonies,' he insisted, 'without a germ of hatred being introduced, which will some day or other… develop mischief of the most serious character.' The veteran congressman, Thaddeus Stevens, a vigorous spokesman for the opposition, rounded on the president with bitter rhetoric:

The punishment of traitors has been wholly ignored by a treacherous executive… Strip a proud nobility of the bloated estates; reduce them to a level with plain republicans; send them forth to labour and teach their children to enter the workshops or handle a plough and you will thus humble the proud traitors.

The first contest came in February 1866 over the issue of the Freedmen's Bureau. This important body had been set up immediately after the cessation of hostilities to implement practical reforms in the South and, specifically, to enable ex-slaves to adjust to their new situation as full and equal citizens of the republic. The bureau distributed food to poor white and black people, set up hospitals and schools and operated a bank to provide for the financing of relief operations and the establishment of new commercial enterprises. Alas for good intentions! The bank soon fell into the hands of unscrupulous financiers and collapsed, taking with it the savings of many of those it had been designed to help. However, much of its work continued and its agents could scarcely keep pace with the demands on their services. Particularly, they had to deal with thousands of blacks who were clamouring for education. In February 1866 Congress passed a bill extending the remit of the Freedmen's Bureau. President Johnson took the almost unprecedented step of vetoing the bill. The stunned congressmen discussed the measure further and submitted a revised bill. This, too, the president rejected. Congress would not be denied. They declared the bill enacted, despite presidential opposition. Johnson might have lost a battle but he certainly did not concede ultimate victory. Henceforth, he used every stratagem to negate or delay the implementation of Congress legislation.

In April 1866 the joint committee proposed a new amendment to the constitution (the 14th). 'No state,' it declared, 'shall make or enforce any law which shall abridge the privileges or immunities of citizens of the United States; nor shall any state deprive any person of life, liberty or property, without due process of law; nor deny to any person within its jurisdiction the equal protection of the laws.' On the surface, this was simply a measure to outlaw discriminatory state legislation and guarantee the rights and privileges of the freed slaves, but it had serious implications for the constitution. It extended the powers of Congress in relation to both the presidency and the state legislatures. The committee declared that the recalcitrant state governments were now mere 'disorganised communities without civil government and without constitutions... by virtue of which political relation could legally exist between them and the federal government'. Southern governments now simply ceased to exist or to be represented in the federal assembly, a state of affairs that left Johnson all the more isolated. The humiliating terms to be imposed upon any state requiring readmission to the Union were as follows:

Repeal of race-based legislation
Disqualification from office of all who had been active in the rebellion.
Guarantee of full civil rights for coloured citizens, including the right to vote.
Establishment of 'republican' government – i.e. fully in tune with the ethos of the northern legislatures.

What was demanded was nothing less than conversion; the southern leopards must change their spots. There was no way that was going to happen.

Johnson now pinned his hopes – as did the southerners – on the congressional election of 1866. This became one of the most bitterly fought contests in American history. In public speeches the president denounced Stevens and other campaigners for Negro rights, claimed that they were planning to assassinate him and even suggested that his opponents deserved to be strung up on the nearest gallows. Electioneering always brings out the worst in participants, but the supposedly democratic campaign of 1866 ranks among the most appalling in the political history of the Western world. Weeks of heated campaigning and frequent news of fresh atrocities in the South played into the hands of the extremists, who gained a two-thirds majority in both houses. Thus empowered, the extremists pushed through a series of measures designed to rub the southerners' noses in their defeat.

But it was not in the corridors of power that the real tragedies of 1865–6 were being enacted. As officials and businessmen from the North set about the task of overseeing reconstruction, they encountered a sullen and obstructive white population. They often made the situation worse for themselves. Federal agents could be ruthless in exacting retribution. Under orders to raise revenue for the central administration, they confiscated crops and land from farmers for non-payment of taxes. The leaders of the nation urged moderation and restraint in the interests of restoring harmony, but their underlings were less disposed to be charitable. Their conviction was that the cotton barons had brought trouble on themselves and must be made to pay for their misdeeds. Six million acres of land in Mississippi were confiscated by the men from Washington. Later, when more sensible policies prevailed, the government was obliged to repay no less than 40,000 claimants for property unjustly confiscated in the heady days of retribution. At the same time northern businessmen discerned opportunities for great profit in the stricken South. Opportunists arrived in large numbers to buy up cheap land, open businesses, sell imported articles at inflated prices and establish themselves as prominent citizens. Many of them were bankrupts, criminals, charlatans and other adventurers who had been unsuccessful in their own home towns and who realised that the South was a sellers' market with little or no local competition. These get-rich-quick merchants earned for themselves the contemptuous nickname of 'carpetbaggers', men who arrived with empty valises intending to stuff them with southern 'loot'. The term was soon being applied to all Yankee (i.e. northern) immigrants.

This was not entirely fair; many officials and entrepreneurs came with the best of intentions but, in the poisoned post-war atmosphere, all strangers were tarred with the same brush. This misrepresentation applied on both sides of the divide. Margaret Mitchell, in her immensely popular novel dealing with the disruption of southern life, *Gone With the Wind,* described popular reaction to the election of a northern Republican as Georgia's state governor:

> If the capture of Georgia by Sherman had caused bitterness, the final capture of the state's capitol by the Carpetbaggers, Yankees, and negroes caused an intensity of bitterness such as the state had never known before. Atlanta and Georgia seethed and raged… But far and above the anger at waste, mismanagement and graft was the resentment of the people at the bad light in which the governor

represented them in the North. When Georgia howled against corruption, the governor hastily went North, appeared before Congress and told of white outrages against negroes, of Georgia's preparation for another rebellion and the need for stern military rule in the state... All Georgia wanted was to be left alone so the state could recuperate. But with the operation of what came to be known as the governor's 'slander mill', the North saw only a rebellious state that needed a heavy hand.

Bad as things might be economically and politically, at least members of the ex-slave population had freedom and the chance of a brighter future, hadn't they? In a word: No. By the end of 1865 slavery had been pronounced illegal and all US citizens had been declared equal before the law. At a stroke some four million coloured people in the South were granted civil rights. It was the biggest act of liberation in history. The next, inevitable step concerned the black franchise. The radical majority in Congress were determined to force the ex-Confederate states to grant full voting rights to ex-slaves and their descendants. And this despite the fact that in 1865, blacks only enjoyed the right to vote in six of the northern states! The idea was anathema to most southern whites. Civil rights might have been granted legally but no law could change the way the white population of the Confederate states thought about their former slaves.

> We should treat them as mere grown-up children, entitled, like children or apprentices, to the protection of guardians or masters and bound to obey those put above them in place of parents, just as children are so bound.

So wrote one southern newspaper, accurately encapsulating the superior white attitude that had prevailed in plantation society for generations. As for the Negroes themselves, many were just plain confused. They left the estates where they had grown up. Whole families went on the road in search of the new destiny they thought emancipation had won for them. Some actually believed that the social order would be turned upside down; that they would now become the masters, living in the big houses and driving around in fancy carriages. What they discovered was unemployment, poverty and a lack of that security that the old order, for all its evils, had given them. Thousands of vagrant ex-slaves died of starvation in the first year of peace.

Misapprehension and disappointed hopes had been fed by the ad hoc handling of an urgent problem in the closing stages of the war. As the victorious northern armies swept through the plantation lands, tens of thousands of displaced ex-slaves had thronged the military camps expecting their liberators to provide for them. General William Sherman came up with a sweeping solution – 'forty acres and a mule'. Land along the Georgia coast and nearby islands was allocated for Afro-American settlement in plots large enough to sustain a family. These ill-conceived societies were little more than ghettoes. Within them, Sherman decreed,

> No white person whatever, unless military officers and soldiers detailed for duty, will be permitted to reside; and the sole and exclusive management of affairs will be left to the freed people themselves, subject only to the United States military authority and the acts of Congress. By the laws of war and orders of the President of the United States, the negro is free and must be dealt with as such... Domestic servants, blacksmiths, carpenters and other mechanics will be free to select their own work and residence, but the young and able-bodied negroes must be encouraged to enlist as soldiers in the service of the United States, to contribute their share towards maintaining their own freedom and securing their rights as citizens of the United States.

By June 1865 10,000 freed slaves had been settled under Sherman's scheme. Later that same year President Johnson rescinded the order and restored the confiscated lands to their original white owners. Small wonder that the phrase 'forty acres and a mule' has become a byword in America for broken government promises. But it would be more realistic to understand the fate of the Sherman plan as the failure that almost inevitably follows from the application of high principles which takes no account of political realities.

The governments of the southern states made some concessions to the changed status of their Afro-American populations. They brought into being what were called 'black codes'. These differed from state to state but were all intended as compromises to define more precisely the rights of ex-slaves. In no state did these include the right to vote. The black codes were quite unacceptable to the congressional radicals, who stepped up their crusade to enforce full racial equality. In the view of the southern leaders some such pragmatic solutions were vital if an increasingly ugly situation was to be brought under control. The vast majority of black men were now competing in the job market with poor whites. This could only fuel race hatred. Every ex-slave who found work was seen as an interloper taking the bread from the mouths of his social superiors. To desperate and resentful displaced white farmers and tradesmen, it seemed obvious that the blacks and the 'nigger-loving do-gooders' of the North were the instigators of all their woes.

Humiliation, frustration and desperation needed an outlet, needed scapegoats and many were ready to hand. In May 1866 a white mob burned down the Negro quarter of Memphis, killing forty-six inhabitants and maiming countless others. In July a gang of New Orleans louts, including several police, attacked a meeting of negroes and their supporters, shooting and sabring scores of unarmed men in cold blood. Violence to individuals was a daily occurrence. Black men and women who presumed to give expression to their new equality, for example by refusing to doff their hats to their 'betters', were roughly handled. Few offenders were brought to book for these outrages, which became increasingly common.

Beyond these spontaneous outbreaks of race hatred lay something altogether more sinister. What the leaders of southern society feared above all was the achievement of political power by the blacks and their sympathisers. In states where the traditionalists were outnumbered it was obvious that their opponents would gain and main-tain the upper hand through the workings of the democratic process. It was, therefore, necessary to prevent the working of the democratic process. To obstruct this, reactionary activists resorted to extra-constitutional methods. Thus were born the secret societies or *kuklos*. Like the Nazi SS brigades, the Spanish Inquisition courts and other inhuman organisations that tend to be thrown up at times of deep ideological crisis, these groups existed for one purpose only – intimidation. Men not approved by the supremacists had to be prevented at all costs from running for office or exercising their right to vote. The *kuklos* indulged in violence of every kind – murder, rape, arson, beatings and all manner of threatening behaviour.

One former slave, subsequently a member of the Georgian state legislature, later recalled for the benefit of a congressional committee how he had been treated by a white mob. His house, he said, was raided at dead of night.

> They took me out of bed, took me to the woods and whipped me three hours or more and left me for dead. They said to me, 'Do you think you will ever vote another damned Radical ticket?'… They had their pistols and they took me in my night clothes … They told me to take off my shirt. I said, 'I never do that for any man. My drawers fell down about my feet and they took hold of them and tripped me up… About two days before they whipped me they offered me $5,000 to go with them [i.e. to vote on their side] and said they would pay me $2,500 in cash if I would let another man go to the legislature in my place… My mother, wife and daughter were in the room when they came. My little daughter begged them not to carry me away. They drew out a

gun and actually frightened her to death. She never got over it until she died. That was the part that grieves me the most.

Although they laid their plans in secret, the white bully boys held authority in contempt and were not above flaunting themselves in lurid rituals involving firelit ceremonies, semi-religious costumes and blood oaths. The most notorious of these societies was the Ku Klux Klan, whose members dressed up in masked hoods and white robes as they gathered around large burning crosses for their elaborate nocturnal rallies, but the KKK was far from being the only such racist militia. By the end of 1866 a state of terror prevailed in several areas of the South. It would continue for many years. As far as government representation was concerned, these tactics were abundantly successful. In not one of the southern states did blacks attain a presence that in any way corresponded with their numbers.

If brutality occurred and if local authorities turned a blind eye to it, it was not just because the former slave owners resented the uprooting of their old, comfortable lifestyle. It was because they were told by their preachers that it was their God-given right and duty to keep dark-skinned people in subjection. The southern racial supremacists could only see Washington's plans for the future as turning the created order upside down. To them it was a simple fact of life that black people *were* inferior and could not possibly assume control of the state or even contribute intelligently to its development. But behind such pseudo-religious reasoning lay the fear of how liberated slaves would handle power. After decades of being beaten into submission by their owners, what would happen if they were now put on an equal footing with their masters and, specifically, given the right to bear arms? The only way they could see to prevent the underclass from taking revenge for generations of ill-treatment was to make sure – whatever the law said – that white folk kept the upper hand. Then there was the question of employment. The southern authorities were responsible for maintaining law and order, and one factor that threatened it was competition for jobs between poor whites and ex-slaves. When their whole world was falling about their ears it is understandable (though inexcusable) that bloodlust should prevail among the unemployed and should be vented on those who seemed to be taking the honest bread from the mouths of lower-class families. As one early commentator observed, the only thing shared among all southerners was misery.

White men, too, were victims of lawless violence and in all portions of the North as well as in the late 'rebel' states. Not a political campaign passed without the exchange of bullets, the breaking of skulls with sticks and stones, the firing of rival club-houses. Republican clubs marched the streets of Philadelphia amid revolver shots and brickbats to save the negroes from the 'rebel' savages in Alabama... The project to make voters out of black men was not so much for their social elevation as for the further punishment of the Southern white people – for the capture of offices for Radical scamps and the entrenchment of the Radical party in power for a long time to come in the South and in the country at large.

No end could be seen to the suffering of all sections of the southern community. Eventually, Congress took the only action that could change the situation in a reasonably short space of time. They imposed military rule. Under the new breed of military governors, harsh and often unjust measures were imposed. Law courts gave way to military tribunals. Radical policies were enforced at gunpoint. It was not good government but it was government – and the only kind which, given the circumstances – could work. When the hyenas of violence were stalking the land, only the violence of the federal lion could deal with them.

The society that emerged from the civil war was born out of hatred and it went on to breed more hatred. Two cultures had clashed and would continue to clash. By the end of 1866 only one of the eleven rebel states – Johnson's Tennessee – had been readmitted to the Union. It would be another four years before the last breakaway state, Mississippi, was reconciled. The constitutional stalemate in Washington continued as Congress passed 'Reconstruction' laws and the president did his utmost to frustrate them. Matters came to a head in 1868 when articles of impeachment were brought against Johnson and failed ony by one vote.

The problems facing what might reasonably be called the 'Disunited States of America' would not be solved in one presidential term, or one decade, or even one century. The civil rights agitation which disturbed the nation in the 1960s had its roots in the conflict of the 1860s. Some historians have called the federal legislation that then finally outlawed racial segregation and ensured equal rights for all American citizens the 'Second Reconstruction'. So emotionally charged are the issues raised by this appalling episode in the nation's history that there is no consensus among historians on what it was all about, where blame is to be placed, or whether the crisis could have been avoided. It rarely happens that there is such a fundamental clash of cultures within one nation. If the southern states had been allowed to go their own way, it would probably have led to greater fragmentation. The West and the Midwest might well have found other reasons to throw off the federal yoke. Certainly the Confederate states would have had to abandon slavery sooner or later if they wanted to keep their place among civilised nations. If Congress had not been so obsessed with principles and had, instead of granting full political rights to freed blacks, concentrated on improving their material well-being and education, gradual integration might have proved possible.

But history does not consist of 'what ifs'. The failure of the Reconstruction, even more than the civil war itself, speaks to us eloquently about the nature of mid-nineteenth-century North America. Failure was inevitable because the ideological rift in society was wide and the Union constitution was unable to bridge it. That it should have happened when it did is not surprising. Territorial expansion focused attention on the slavery issue and forced it to the top of the agenda. But there is a certain irony about the timing of the showdown. In the middle of the nineteenth century the USA was emerging as the proud champion of prosperity, progress and, above all, democracy.

> Thou, too, sail on, O Ship of State!
> Sail on, O Union, strong and great!
> Humanity with all its fears,

With all the hopes of future years,
Is hanging breathless on thy fate.

So wrote the American poet, Henry Wadsworth Longfellow, in 1849, and he wasn't exaggerating. To many people in a Europe torn by a multitude of little wars, political protests and revolutions, where human freedoms were being systematically crushed by autocratic regimes, there seemed to be a golden glow on the western horizon. North America was *the* land of promise. Migrants were crossing the Atlantic in ever-increasing numbers. Just as the founders of the nation had fled from oppression in the seventeenth century, so these new refugees were seeking a new life in an open society radiant with promise. They were travelling to an 'empty' continent where, so they believed, their talents and industry would pay dividends and where no state controls would impose limits on their success; where there were no class divisions and where they would have a say in the political life of their chosen land. America was a nation carrying 'the hopes of future years'. It was, above all, the land of the free.

Men and women disembarking on the east coast did not take very long to discover the flaws in that vision. They heard tub-thumpers ardently promoting anti-slavery campaigns. New arrivals with heads full of political idealism were easily recruited to the cause. Clashes were not infrequent, some of them violent. In 1831 an insurrection in Virginia led to the death of fifty-seven white people and reprisals against a hundred or so blacks. Sympathisers in the North operated a 'black railroad', smuggling runaways from the plantations into free northern society. Southern leaders blamed the anti-slavery agitation for encouraging disaffection and demanded the suppression of liberation literature and preaching. All the time the slave population in the South was increasing and with it the anxiety of white owners. It was clear that the storm could not be long in breaking. When it did, the world witnessed a war between two of the largest armies in known history. Many men who had fled turmoil in Italy or Germany ended up shedding their blood in the land of the free.

Then, in 1865–6, came failed Reconstruction and the realisation that the war had not solved the problem but had, on the contrary, added to it. Attitudes had hardened. Free, democratic America gave birth to terrorist organisations every bit as bestial as those which threaten modern Western society. And an extremist federal government employed autocratic and constitutionally dubious methods to coerce the South. How many recent immigrants, one wonders, were disillusioned by the reality of the brave new society they had travelled thousands of miles to join?

Chapter 8

1942-3

Our army was retreating, abandoning our native villages and towns in Ukraine, Byelorussia, Moldavia, the Leningrad region, the Baltic region, and the Karelo-Finnish Republic, abandoning them because there was no other alternative. Another people might have said to the government, 'You have not come up to our expectation. Get out. We shall appoint another government, which will conclude peace with Germany and ensure tranquillity for us.' But the Russian people did not do that... and they made sacrifices in order to ensure the defeat of Germany. And this... proved to be the decisive factor which ensured our historic victory over the enemy of mankind. Over fascism.

Joseph Stalin

Anyone who has stood in front of the Monument to the Heroic Defenders of Leningrad in modern St Petersburg cannot fail to be moved by the story it tells. A forty-eight-metre-high obelisk towers over monumental sculpture depicting the men and women who withstood the longest siege in the history of recent times. But it is in the underground memorial hall that vivid images of shattered buildings and broken bodies tell the story of that most incredibly feat of endurance: the siege of Leningrad. For 900 days this beautiful city withstood the attempts of a ferocious enemy to obliterate it and to crush its people. Leningrad survived and the memorial stands at the closest point reached by the invaders. But the cost was horrendous. Starvation, disease and injury reduced the population from four million to two and a half million. Dogged resistance in Leningrad and other Soviet cities did, as Stalin later said, ensure the ultimate defeat of Nazi Germany. From the Baltic to the Black Sea, the advance of the invaders was halted. The refusal of the inhabitants of this large area to surrender meant that the would-be conquerors were bogged down and subjected to harsh eastern European winters. They lost tens of thousands of troops and the survivors were in poor shape to continue the fight when the Soviet army was ready for a counter-offensive. But was the price of survival the monster Stalin forced his fellow countrymen to pay too high?

In 1939 the German Führer, Adolf Hitler, agreed a non-aggression pact with Stalin's government. There was no love lost between the two regimes;

quite the reverse. Hitler considered the extirpation of Communism to be the principal objective of his political crusade and Stalin's loathing of Nazism was just as profound. The two leaders embodied the prejudices that had beset their nations for centuries. Hitler entertained a passionate hatred of the 'inferior' Slav peoples and believed that their only value was as slaves to assist in the spread of pure, Aryan civilisation. Stalin's political creed was based on traditional suspicion of the West and on Karl Marx's theory of the inevitable triumph of the proletariat over the forces of international capitalism, which Germany now represented. Both national leaders believed that war between them was only a matter of time but a truce suited them both.

Germany had, over the previous three years ,added Czechoslovakia and Austria to its empire, while the other Western nations looked on and did nothing. Hitler's eyes were now fixed on Poland, France, the Low Countries and Norway. With the Soviet Union quiescent, he could concentrate all his resources on the Western Front.

Stalin's aggressive intentions were just as clear: if the Western democracies had their hands full with Hitler, they would be unable to prevent the Soviet Union 'adjusting' its own frontiers. Over the following months eastern Poland, Latvia, Lithuania, Estonia, Bessarabia and part of Finland were occupied by Soviet troops. With scarcely a shot being fired, Stalin had created a Russian empire bigger than the land mass over which the tsars had presided. Ironically, Stalin thought that by pushing Soviet frontiers farther to the west he was reducing the possibility of a German invasion. He believed he had plenty of time to prepare his defences while Hitler occupied himself elsewhere.

He underestimated the might of the German war machine. Hitler's *Blitzkrieg* tactics (rapid advance with vastly superior land and air military might) carried his armies right up to the Atlantic coast within months. Only offshore Britain was left, making defiant noises but inevitably just as doomed as Holland, Belgium and France had been. In 1940–1 the Nazi leader tried, unsuccessfully, to bomb Britain into submission. Then, instead of expending more resources on a cross-Channel invasion, he radically changed his strategy. He decided to switch his main attack to the USSR. He saw no reason why *Blitzkrieg* should not be just as effective in the East as in the West. In June 1941 he launched Operation Barbarossa, a spectacular armoured assault involving three and a half million men. This was by far the biggest army ever assembled in all European history. Not since the devastating hordes of Attila the Hun had swept before them the legions of Rome in the fifth century had anything comparable been seen in terms of rapid and destructive advance. Hitler exulted in the overwhelming military power he wielded and believed implicitly that he could crush all opposition. His conviction was that quick victory in the East would make Britain and her potential ally, the USA, realise that further resistance was pointless. Thus the Third Reich would achieve the world domination that was its destiny.

With hindsight we can see that Hitler and Stalin possessed similar mentalities. Neither was a military tactician but both assumed personal direction of their armies at crucial stages of the war. Both believed in sheer force and were indifferent to human suffering, whether inflicted on the enemy or endured by their own people. Obsessed by their own ideologies, they pursued policies that ultimately brought about the collapse of the very systems they sought to impose on large areas of Europe.

By the end of 1941 the Germans had bulldozed their way through hundreds of kilometres of Soviet territory and established a line from Leningrad in the north to Rostov on the Black Sea. But they had not achieved their first objective of crushing the USSR before the onset of winter. Soviet resistance was stronger than Hitler had imagined it would be. Stalin was as bull-headed as his enemy in demanding of his people every sacrifice in the defence of their homeland. At the same time he actually helped his adversary by being just as tactically blinkered. His generals asked for reinforcements from army units in the Far East. Stalin not only rejected this appeal, he sacked his chief of staff for suggesting it. As the two military juggernauts clashed, casualties on both sides were on an appalling scale. Germany lost a million men in the first stage of the offensive. Neither army took prisoners. Civilians were shot indiscriminately. Hitler did send more units eastwards, along with his personal instructions: there must be no turning back, not even tactical retreat. A major failing of the German leader was his obsessive belief that all other peoples were inferior to his Aryan master race. This attitude prevented him from forming alliances with the governments of the nations he was 'liberating'. There were plenty of anti-communists in Russia and the Soviet satellites with whom Hitler might have done deals. They could have supplied him with additional troops and military equipment. By blasting his way across their territory he convinced them that life under Nazi rule would be no better than that under the Soviet regime with its secret police, rigid economic control and labour camps. Central Europe was presented with a choice between two inhuman regimes.

Militarily there were two important differences between these mighty combatants. Germany possessed the biggest and best-equipped land and air forces in the world. Though the Nazis were superior in terms of trained troops, the Soviet Union held two advantages – advantages that had enabled Russia to see off previous invasions over the centuries: its territory extended over thousands and thousands of square kilometres to the east and its human resources were almost limitless. The USSR could draw upon vast reserves of manpower. Perhaps we might add a third advantage: the Soviet people had an almost suicidal tenacity. The story is told of an earlier conflict between Russia and Prussia. The Prussians held an apparently impregnable position but the Russians attacked again and again and again. They stumbled over the bodies of their fallen comrades and refused to call off their assault while the Prussians kept up a relentless fire and looked on in disbelief. Sheer fanatical persistence won the day and when, after the battle, the defeated Prussian commander asked his opposite number how he could justify sending so many of his men to be slaughtered, the Russian officer replied with a shrug: 'There are many of them.'

When the Soviet government woke up to the urgency of their predicament, they made the most of their natural advantages. By the end of 1941 they had moved two and a half million troops up to the front line and evacuated from the area vulnerable to attack one and a half million railway truckloads of heavy machinery, which was then installed in new factories for the production of armaments in the Urals, western Siberia and Kazakhstan. In December MiG fighters and T-34 tanks began rolling off the assembly lines. It was not only military personnel and heavy machines that were moved. Stalin was well aware that there were in the empire he ruled disaffected people who might be tempted to go over to the enemy. So he transported them – lock, stock and barrel. Tatars, Chechens, Kalmyks, Karachais – families, farming communities, whole villages were summarily uprooted. Folk whose ancestors had been domiciled on their land for generations were packed onto eastbound trains and deposited in Siberia.

There were three targets of particular strategic importance for the invaders: Leningrad, which controlled Soviet access to the Baltic; Moscow, the capital; and, farther south, Stalingrad, the gateway to the Caucasus with its important oilfields. Stalin was determined to balk the invaders – at all points. There was no finesse to his strategy. He did not choose priority targets or concentrate on breaking the Germans' over-extended supply lines. He fought along the whole front. His strategy, if such it can be called, was simply to confront the Nazi machine with a human wall against which it would break itself. And he had the manpower resources to do just that. By the spring of 1942 he was able to mobilise six million troops. When the Germans got within thirty-five kilometres of Moscow, the government retreated to a town 800 kilometres farther east. But they left orders that Russia's principal city was to be defended at all costs and, thanks to the frenzied determination of the Soviet army, the German advance was halted some twenty-seven kilometres short of the capital. Stalin and the politburo were back in Moscow by the end of the year. Now it was the invaders' turn to suffer. They had been sent eastwards to gain a quick summer and autumn victory. They had not been equipped with the clothing and other essential supplies to cope with the Russian winter. The bitter cold of the next three months sapped their energy and only the manic orders of the Führer terrified the generals into sitting it out until the warmer weather. In fact, Hitler's *Blitzkrieg* plan unravelled within a year of its launch and he had no other with which to replace it. All he could do was urge his troops to keep pressing forward. With determined and all-powerful dictators controlling the action and often overruling the counsels of their generals on the spot, the conflict on the Eastern Front became a war of attrition. That meant that it became a long, drawn-out hell for the civilian population. This period, 1942–3, the central phase of what Russian historians call the 'Great Patriotic War', was a time of suffering, scarcely imaginable for millions of Soviet people.

The Battle of Stalingrad lasted from 17 July 1942 to 2 February 1943 and in those few months almost two million people – civilians as well as military personnel – were killed. The offensive proved to be another example of *Blitzkrieg* not quite achieving its objective. German aerial bombardment and artillery fire rapidly reduced three-quarters of the city to mounds of rubble, but did not overcome the tenacity of the defenders. Stalin's determination that Stalingrad was not to be abandoned was as rigid as Hitler's determination that it must be captured.

Soviet tactics were brutal in their simplicity. Stalingrad was to be the rock upon which the Nazi axe would fall and be blunted. The government ordered as much food as possible to be shipped eastwards to feed the soldiers who were to hold the invaders in check. At the same time civilians were prevented from evacuating the city in order to augment the military presence. Old people, women and children were set to work digging trenches and building barriers while death rained down from the skies. Soldiers whose nerve broke or who were dubbed cowards by the security police were shot *pour encourager les autres*. Around 14,000 people are said to have been killed in this way on the orders of their known leaders. Troop reinforcements were shipped across the River Volga in barges, which were soon targeted by the German air force with appalling effectiveness. As the invaders worked their way through the suburbs and entered the broken city under cover of the bombardment, Soviet commanders hampered their advance by maintaining as close contact as possible with the enemy. This obliged the Germans and their Hungarian, Romanian and Italian allies to rely on close-quarter fighting; air and artillery support was rendered useless by the risk of injury to their own troops. Soviet officers in charge of anti-tank guns deployed on the other side of the Volga were less hesitant about firing. Every rooftop, every street corner, every hastily constructed barricade became the location for machine-gun posts, sniper units and mortar positions. Even the sewers were used to move defenders rapidly from point to point. Twentieth-century warfare had become largely a mechanised business in which death and destruction could be launched at long range with reduced need for hand-to-hand combat. The fighting in the streets of Stalingrad was a return to old-style, vicious confrontation in which combatants, driven by fear and hatred, faced each other before squeezing a trigger or throwing a hand grenade. There were even instances of enemy troops occupying the same building and firing at each other through holes in floors and ceilings.

Throughout the autumn the Nazis advanced at snail's pace, contesting every metre of ground and suffering terrible losses. One position – a railway station – changed hands fourteen times in six hours. Another location proved impregnable: defenders had to remove German corpses from the walls in order to gain an unimpeded field of fire. Meanwhile, the Soviet government was building up its military strength. As well as the planes and vehicles turned out by their own factories, they were receiving supplies from their allies. The USA was shipping in trucks, jeeps, shells and even boots. As house-to-house fighting took over from attempted obliteration, the invaders lost their advantage. Not only did ruined buildings provide excellent cover for the defending troops, streets clogged with piles of bricks and masonry prevented the German tanks and armoured vehicles advancing.

As autumn turned to winter the invading troops found themselves ill-equipped to face its rigours. This would have been the obvious time for the Nazi commanders to organise a strategic withdrawal and regrouping, a strategy categorically forbidden by Berlin. In September Hitler had delivered a speech to his devoted followers in which he promised that his armies would never retreat from Stalingrad. When the German chief of staff criticised the strategy, Hitler sacked him. In November the Red Army unleashed its counter-offensive, code-named Operation Uranus. This involved simultaneous attacks from the north and south, directed at poorly equipped Italian, Hungarian and Romanian units. The attackers now became the defenders, the besiegers, the besieged. The Soviet ring around Stalingrad tightened, trapping 290,000 enemy troops and also thousands of Russian military and civilian prisoners. The German air force tried to run a relief operation delivering vital supplies to the starving and freezing troops. It was totally inadequate and badly planned (one plane actually arrived carrying vodka and lightweight uniforms). Over 500 relief planes were destroyed by Soviet aircraft and ground-to-air fire. While German officers tried to keep up the morale of their men with promises that relief columns were on the way, an increasing number died of malnutrition, frostbite and disease as they huddled together in the snow-covered ruins of the city that they, themselves, had destroyed.

As the circle closed the position of those in the city became more desperate by the day. In mid-January the Soviet commander-in-chief offered reasonable terms for a German surrender. They were refused. Many of the invaders preferred to die fighting than to trust the promises of the enemy. They were right to be suspicious. On 2 February 1943 the inevitable end came and 91,000 German and allied troops laid down their arms. They were put to work by their captors rebuilding the city or were shipped to labour camps elsewhere. Most of them did not survive their ordeal. Within a month 40,000 were buried in a mass grave, victims of typhus. Some of the survivors were detained until 1955, ten years after the end of the war. It has been calculated that of the 91,000 Stalingrad captives, only 5,000 ever returned home.

While Stalingrad was undergoing its ordeal, 1,600 kilometres to the north, the defenders of Leningrad were suffering a worse fate. St Petersburg, as it was originally called and as it was later renamed, was a beautiful city, founded by Peter the Great at the beginning of the eighteenth century, much embellished by later tsars and boasting many fine churches, palaces, museums and public buildings. Hitler had no desire to destroy the architectural gems of Leningrad and the priceless artworks contained in the Hermitage and other great collections. He would simply 'liberate' them from their bondage to the inferior Slavs and add this historic city to the other jewels in his Aryan crown. Leningrad was to be surrounded and given a taste of German firepower. It would then 'fall like a leaf'. German planes dropped propaganda leaflets on the city urging its people to surrender in order to avoid the horrors of a full-blown assault. Hitler was so certain of the city's immediate collapse that he issued invitations to a celebration party to be held in Leningrad's premier hotel. That was in June 1941, before the start of Operation Barbarossa. On 29 September the German leader issued Directive 1601: 'The Führer has ordered the city of Leningrad to be wiped off the face of the earth… It is proposed to establish a tight blockade of the city and, by shelling it with artillery of all calibres and incessant bombing, level it to the ground.' The chilling corollary was added that Hitler felt no necessity to avoid mass killing of the civilian population.

Two things seem to have changed his mind. Losses elsewhere on the front, particularly the approaches to Moscow, were heavier than expected and progress was not swift enough. His strategy demanded a quick, successful summer campaign. Hitler did not want the eastern war to drag on into the winter. Now he considered it important for Leningrad to become an object lesson. Russia's second city must be smashed as a warning to the Soviet Union to abandon its futile resistance. Over the 900 days of the siege millions of tons of bombs and shells rained down on the city.

By this time Leningrad was filling up with refugees. Hundreds of thousands of men, women and children were streaming into the city as their towns and villages farther west were overrun. Strict food rationing was enforced as the authorities tried to cope with a much-increased population. Even so, food supplies were soon depleted. The attackers deliberately targeted warehouses containing grain, sugar and other foodstuffs. Water mains were frequently fractured. The authorities calculated that the supply of many basic food-stuffs would be completely exhausted within a month. The situation had been made even worse by an order from Stalin in August that all essential supplies be collected up and sent to Moscow. By mid-September the Germans were within fifteen kilometres of the city and had ringed it completely. They kept up a constant aerial bombardment. As well as food depots, the city's power stations were put out of action. The civilian population faced the prospect of living through the severe Baltic winter without light or heat and with the barest minimum of food. By the end of 1941 more than 350 people a day were dying of starvation. Those with the energy hunted down dogs, cats and rats. The city government experimented with 'alternative' food. 'Bread' might be concocted from rye, oats, barley, cottonseed and the totally non-nutritious cellulose to be found in a variety of plants. 'Soup' might consist of boiled-up weeds, root vegetables and animal guts. Factory workers ate the grease from machine bearings and drank industrial oil. There were even reports of cannibalism. And this was only the beginning of the siege.

Winter came to the aid of the beleaguered citizens. Lake Ladoga froze over, enabling truck-loads of supplies to reach Leningrad. Most of them came from the railway terminus at Tikhvin, 150 kilometres to the east. This had been captured by the Germans but was retaken after a fierce battle in December. As elsewhere, Hitler's 'invincible' army was suffering from being ill-equipped to face the Russian winter. Seven thousand troops died trying to defend Tikhvin. The frozen lake opened up a means of escape for several citizens, but the authorities tried to put a stop to indiscriminate evacuation because they wanted all able-bodied people to stay and maintain some semblance of the essential services. In 1942 a system was in place. Priority was given to technicians and factory personnel who were needed in the industrial centres that were being set up farther east to produce munitions. After them, women and children were moved out. As they crossed the lake, by boat in summer, on foot in winter, they had to run the gauntlet of enemy bombing.

During 1942 the population decreased by around one and a half million. This figure is made up of those who left or who died of starvation, hypothermia or disease. Coping with the dead had gone beyond the control of the authorities. Bodies lay in the streets, covered in snow, because there was no one to bury them. The ground was too hard for the digging of graves. This problem was solved by the use of explosives. Craters were blasted out to make mass graves. 'You can't imagine what it was like,' one survivor later recalled,

> You just stepped over corpses in the streets and on the stairs. You simply stopped taking any notice. It was no use worrying. Terrible things used to happen. Some people went quite insane with hunger. And the practice of hiding the dead somewhere in the

house and using their ration cards was very common indeed. There were so many people dying all over the place authorities couldn't keep track of all the deaths.

The city rulers tried to stop the practice of illegally used ration cards by offering extra food to anyone handing in the documents of someone who had died. One poet wrote tersely: 'Living in Leningrad is like sleeping in a coffin.'

A few citizens, with nothing to do but queue for their meagre ration of bread, kept diaries. This is a typical entry written in the winter of 1942:

The entire flat is appallingly cold, everywhere is frozen... the bleakness of desolation everywhere. The water supply is non-existent, we have to fetch water from more than three kilometres away. The sewage system is a thing of the distant past – the yard is full of muck. This is like some other city, not Leningrad, always so proud of its European, dandyish appearance. To see it now is like meeting a man you have become accustomed to seeing dressed in a magnificent, thick woollen overcoat, sporting clean gloves, a fresh collar, and good American boots. And here you suddenly meet that same man completely transformed – clothed in tatters, filthy, unshaven, with foul-smelling breath and a dirty neck, with rags on his feet instead of boots.

The early months of 1942 were the worst of the siege. The bombardment was at its heaviest and hope at its lowest ebb. The food ration was 300 grams of ersatz bread per child and 500 grams per adult. People spent much of their time huddled together in underground shelters. By night citizen patrols kept a watch for incendiaries and dealt with fires. Many employed on these night watches were children, hundreds of whom died carrying out this dangerous task. Of these days a military officer recalled:

> ...during that winter I don't think I ever saw a person smile. It was frightful. And yet there was a kind of inner discipline that made people carry on. A new code of manners was evolved by the hungry people. They carefully avoided talking about food.

Something that gave the defenders hope was war news brought to them by radio. The repulse of the Germans from Moscow that winter was a welcome boost to morale. But there were worse horrors for the people of Leningrad to face before they could see real light at the end of the tunnel. In March, a new enemy, whose approach the authorities had long feared, made its presence known. Cholera. Bomb-shattered hospitals and desperately overworked medical staff had to cope with an epidemic that was adding hundreds to the daily death count. Doctors and nurses risked infection themselves. The Germans, supplied with maps by spies and fifth columnists, deliberately targeted hospitals. Their infiltrators started fires and poisoned water supplies. Amazingly, the medics coped. By the end of May the outbreak had been contained. But by the time the siege was over half of the doctors and nurses were dead. April saw the heaviest bombardment of the war. The German air force launched Operation Ice Impact, an intensified bombing programme that highlighted not only the brave resistance of the besieged, but also the growing desperation of the besiegers. As the brief northern summer appeared every available space in the city was turned over to vegetable growing. Produce was collected up by the authorities for distribution on an organised basis. This provided a valuable supplement to the diet, but there was no means of preserving vegetables far into the winter.

Pressure on available food supplies was being eased by evacuation. With the passing of time the authorities became more expert at identifying and utilising escape roots. Most of these involved getting weak (and therefore slow) people to and across Lake Ladoga. Throughout 1942 over 400,000 people were evacuated but there is no means of knowing how many of these subsequently survived. The escape operation posed a problem for those in charge of Leningrad's defence. On the one hand there was less pressure on the available food supply. On the other there were fewer people available to maintain the defence of the city. This was vital to Stalin's overall strategy. He needed to keep as many Germans as possible tied up in the attack on Leningrad and, therefore, unable to be diverted to other theatres of war.

Almost as bad as the human suffering was the cultural devastation. Old St Petersburg was one of the most beautiful cities in Europe. It was created from scratch by Peter the Great at the end of the seventeenth century as the new Russian capital and embellished with royal and aristocratic palaces and impressive public buildings. Later tsars employed Europe's leading architects to add other Baroque and Rococo architectural gems to the squares, avenues and waterfront embankments. In deliberate rivalry with extravagant monarchs such as Louis XIV and Frederick the Great, they filled them with paintings and sculptures by leading Western artists. Exteriors were graced with classical pillars and cornices and painted in pastel colours to brighten their appearance during the long, sunless winters. Interiors were exuberant with gilding, mirrors, glittering chandeliers, patterned floors, painted ceilings and elegant furniture. Because the centre of the city took shape over a comparatively short period of time, St Petersburg was a veritable expression of the European Enlightenment. Piety added fine churches and monasteries with gleaming golden domes and needle spires. As one guidebook explains, in its tsarist heyday, 'St Petersburg looked more like a stage set than a working city, with broad avenues built for parades and palaces like props for some grandiose drama'. This cultural richness extended into the suburbs where St Petersburg's elite built their summer palaces. Here were the magnificent Peterhof, conceived as a deliberate imitation of Versailles, and Catherine the Great's Tsarskoye Selo, which boasted the world's longest palace frontage. Such magnificence (mercifully restored) still has the power to take the visitor's breath away.

After the revolution of 1917 Bolshevik and Soviet governments were strangely ambiguous about the city, which was renamed Petrograd, then Leningrad. They despised the tsarist past which it brazenly represented, but maintained a pride in its undeniable splendours. While little money was expended on the upkeep of the palaces and many buildings were turned into office complexes and other more 'useful' buildings, and while Stalin secretly sold off art treasures to mask the failure of his economic plans, few structures were actually allowed to fall into disrepair. The Hermitage, once the winter palace of the tsars, was opened to the public and became one of the world's top ten museums. Its 650,000 works of art included examples of all schools from the Italian and Flemish Renaissance to the Post-Impressionists.

All this became the target for Nazi bombs and artillery shells during the Siege of Leningrad. In the early months of the invasion two thousand museum staff and supporters of the Hermitage packed up hundreds of thousands of art treasures and moved them to safety in the Urals. Other items that could not be easily transported were placed in vaults beneath the Hermitage and St Isaac's Cathedral. Some were even buried. It was a necessary precaution. The Hermitage alone took more than thirty direct hits from enemy fire. Inevitably, many priceless artefacts were lost for all time.

The suburban treasure houses were mercilessly looted. German soldiers suffering from cold chopped up for firewood the furniture and fittings created by great craftsmen and took historic tapestries into the mud of their trenches where they cut them up for makeshift blankets. One example of the rape of Leningrad's heritage is the fate of the Amber Room of Tsarskoye Selo. In the 1750s the Empress Elizabeth commissioned a unique audience room for her palace. Her architect, Bartolomeo Rastrelli, covered the walls of the ninety-six-square-metre salon with panels of amber, interspersed with mirrors and gilded columns. As soon as the war on the Eastern Front began Tsarskoye Selo's more movable treasures were crated up and despatched to Gorky, Novosibirsk and Sarapul, a thousand kilometres and more to the east. But it was not possible to dismantle the amber panels. What the Russian custodians could not do the Germans accomplished in thirty-six hours. They arrived in mid-September 1941, and, by the beginning of November, the walls of Elizabeth's audience chamber were bare. The panels were taken to Königsberg, where they were put on display for the benefit of Hitler's subjects with a sign reading 'Amber Room from Tsarskoye Selo presented to the museum by the German State Administration for palaces and Gardens'. In 1944 the panels were, once again, taken down and hidden away, this time to preserve them from British forces. Königsberg was one of the German cities subjected to heavy bombing by the Allies. What happened to the Tsarskoye Selo masterpiece thereafter remains a mystery. It simply disappeared.

No European city suffered a devastation worse than that of Leningrad during the whole of the Second World War. The London blitz, the bombing of Dresden, the pounding of Berlin – none bears comparison to the obliteration of Russia's second city. The urban wasteland created by German bombs, incendiaries and artillery shells has been compared, with scarce exaggeration, to the flattened cities of Hiroshima and Nagasaki after the dropping of atomic bombs in 1945.

The turning point, although it was not obvious to everyone at the time, came in January 1943. The Germans lost the battle for Stalingrad and their stranglehold on Leningrad was broken. The war was far from over and fortunes would surge back and forth before Hitler's forces were in desperate retreat in the last weeks of the year. German troops were not driven away from Leningrad until January 1944. Then, slowly and, at first, hesitantly, Russians began returning to the shattered city. It would take years, decades, to restore Leningrad to anything like its old appearance and create a modern city with new industries and efficient public services. And even recovery had a sting in its tail. Stalin ordered the arrest of the local leaders who had been responsible for the city's survival. They had shouldered an immense burden and had shown superhuman courage in the face of unimaginable hardship. They had maintained law and order in a situation when all authority might well have broken down. They had taken difficult decisions and acted on their own initiative because no one outside Leningrad could possibly have known, day by day, what was needed. That, apparently, was their crime. They had acted independently of Moscow and they had been successful. Stalin could not permit anyone to share the honours of Soviet victory, let alone threaten to outshine him.

The fate of these unsung heroes in the gulags of Siberia is beyond the scope of the story of 1942–3 but it does underline what happens when two unspeakably awful regimes come into conflict. It is ordinary people that get crushed. The real conflict on the Eastern Front in the Second World War was not between two different styles of totalitarian government, but between authoritarianism and humanitarianism. Hitler and Stalin both headed regimes that set no store by human suffering. They were driven by ideologies which, in turn, were fashioned by old hatreds and resentments. Bolshevism and its later Stalinist manifestation were a reaction to centuries of tsarist autocracy. Nazism was the response of people who had been humiliated in the war of 1914–18. The upholders of both systems were determined to force their own solutions on their own people and, then, on a wider world. But political systems and theories backed by military force, secret police and the techniques of coercion are self-contradictory because they do not exhibit that concern and care for the people they claim to liberate and in whose name they claim to speak. In 1942, far away from Moscow, Stalingrad and Leningrad, a British politician, William Beveridge, was laying out plans for what would become the welfare state. He took it as his foundation principle that 'The object of government in peace and war is not the glory of rulers or of races, but the happiness of the common man'. National leaders may and will disagree about how that object is to be achieved, but the appalling suffering inflicted without a single twinge of conscience upon millions of people in eastern Europe in 1942–3 should stand as a warning to them and to those who vote them into office about what can happen when the 'glory of rulers and races' and the tyranny of ideas are allowed to control international relations.

Chapter 9

1968

To stand on the rostrum at the Olympic Games, to see your country's flag hoisted aloft and to hear your national anthem played must be the proudest moment in any athlete's life. So for a sportsman to choose that moment to actually *criticise* his own nation is guaranteed to shock many people and to gain the headlines. On 16 October 1968, two sprinters stood on the winners' rostrum at the Mexico Olympics. They were Tommie Smith and John Carlos and they had won, for the USA, the gold and bronze medals respectively in the 200 metres final. As the Stars and Stripes flag was raised high in the arena, these two mixed-race athletes held up clenched, black-gloved fists in the black power salute. Within twenty-four hours photographs of this carefully planned snub to the Washington government were on the front pages of newspapers the world over.

That image defined 1968. It was, pre-eminently, the year of protest. In several countries the normal course of life was disrupted by demonstrations. People paraded in the streets, stormed embassies, staged sit-ins, organised mass rallies and went on destructive rampages in opposition to several aspects of contemporary life as organised by the ruling elites. They protested about racial discrimination, sexual inequality, involvement in foreign war, suppression of national identity, university curricula and a raft of political issues. Most of the protestors were young. They were men and women just coming to maturity who had no direct experience of the Second World War. That meant that they did not share passionately the emotions of an older generation who had fought and suffered to protect a way of life they believed in. They felt free – indeed, they felt obliged – to challenge the people in power, people who had been reared on the other side of the 1939–45 cultural divide. What they were saying was: 'This is a new world, our world, and we don't like what you're doing to it'. This generation (at least in the West) had more money, better education and was more widely travelled than any generation that had preceded it. And there was one phenomenon that prevented these diverse demonstrations of unrest being of purely local concern: the development of communications technology. Thanks to the innovation of orbital satellites, news flew around the planet in minutes. Protest became a contagion, spreading rapidly from country to country, city to city. It was *that* which gave 1968 its unique flavour of a world not at ease with itself.

So intermeshed were all these movements and so cumulative their effect that the best way to present them is chronologically. What follows, therefore, is a month-by-month (one might almost say 'blow-by-blow') account of this troubled year.

On 19 January a polite luncheon party was held in the Washington White House. The president's wife, Lady Bird Johnson, was hosting a party for fifty prominent American women. The subject of the speeches they listened to was crime and urban unrest, and the speakers extolled the liberal virtues of firm policing tempered by redress of genuine grievances. Then a diminutive black lady stepped to the lectern. That in itself was something of a novelty, but this Afro-American celebrity was no ordinary person. Her name was Eartha Kitt and she was a stage and cabaret singer of international reputation. She represented what many liberal Americans believed their nation stood for: equal opportunity for all citizens, irrespective of colour, to achieve their full potential. Eartha seemed to be living and breathing proof that the USA was not racist. But, if the audience, well fed with superb food elegantly served, expected some expression of grateful support for the Johnson administration they were in for a shock. The singer had her own take on why young people behaved in disorderly ways on the streets. 'You send the best of this country off to be shot and maimed,' she said. 'They rebel in the streets. They take pot and get high. They don't want to go to school because they're going to be snatched from their mothers to be shot in Vietnam.' That brief speech dramatically brought into alignment the two big issues that were fragmenting American society: opposition to the war and the demand for full civil rights for black Americans.

America had been involved in Vietnam since the French colonial power pulled out in 1954. The communist regime in the North steadily extended its control over the southern part of the country. Successive US administrations, concerned to prevent the 'domino effect' of more and more Asian countries going 'red', had been drawn deeper and deeper into the conflict. By the end of 1967 the war had cost the lives of almost 16,000 combat troops and was gobbling up $2–3 million per month. What made matters worse was that America's youth had no way of avoiding military service because conscription (the 'draft') still existed. With no sign of an end to the war and the government hampered by lack of funds from tackling mounting problems at home, President Johnson's regime was increasingly unpopular – and 1968 was a presidential election year.

Before the month was out, television viewers and newspaper readers were presented with unprecedented graphic images of what the war in Vietnam was really like. Hitherto, government ministers and military chiefs had been able to monitor news coverage of warfare. New technology robbed them of this propaganda advantage and two incidents brought the reality of the Vietnam War into every living room. On 30 January communist guerrillas carried out a suicide raid on the US embassy in the southern capital of Saigon. Press photographs of dead American soldiers and general havoc right at the centre of the American presence in Vietnam raised question marks about the official reportage of the war. Two days later an American press photographer, Eddie Adams, recorded an equally disturbing image. He witnessed and photographed Nguyen Ngoc Loan, a South Vietnamese chief of police, shooting a handcuffed communist prisoner. His picture, syndicated worldwide, rapidly became an icon of the war. In 1969 it would win the Pulitzer Prize. Long before then it had caused many Americans to ask why they were supporting such a regime. In other western countries, closely allied with America since the Second World War, different questions were being asked, as this unpopular war dragged on: Why was this superpower, the traditional champion of democracy and anti-colonial upholder of the rights of all peoples to self-determination, using its military might to prevent Vietnam working out its own salvation? Why was it refusing equality to a large section of its own population? Was its own society falling apart?

The civil rights movement in America had a longer history. As we have seen, for many African-Americans the civil war of 1861–5 brought no relief from their oppression by the white leaders of society. Segregation remained entrenched in most southern states. Successive federal governments had worked to bring state regulations into line with official national policy but progress was slow. By the mid-1950s it had become too slow for many black activists. Protestors challenged authority by sitting in the whites-only seats on buses, in restaurants and other public places and by organising protest marches. The movement had become split between groups dedicated to peaceful protest and organisations countenancing various levels of violence. The acknowledged leader of non-violent resistance was the Reverend Martin Luther King, a Southern Baptist minister with a doctorate from Boston University. King, a born orator, took his inspiration from the Indian nationalist leader Mahatma Gandhi's campaign of civil disobedience. He urged his followers to use passive resistance and to endure suffering rather than be stirred into violent reaction. He was imprisoned thirty times during his active career. King was internationally respected and, in 1964, he became the youngest person ever to receive the Nobel Peace Prize (he was thirty-five). But by 1968 the initiative was being grabbed by extremist groups such as the Black Panthers and

Black Muslims. Even the Student Non-violent Coordinating Committee had been hijacked by 'black power' zealots. In fact, as all organisers had come to realise, what the movement needed was publicity and the most effective way to get press and TV coverage was to generate violence, either by destructive action or by provoking the authorities to brutal counter-measure. On 8 February 1968 a protest rally at a whites-only bowling alley in Orangeville, South Carolina ended with three college students dead. This spurred cantering youth protest into a gallop. The following week student demonstrations disrupted teaching at Wisconsin and North Carolina universities.

At Wisconsin the protestors had planted 400 white crosses on a piece of ground they labelled 'Bascom Memorial Cemetery, Class of 1968' to draw attention to the indisputable fact that several of their friends were, statistically, doomed to being flown back from Asia in coffins. Protest against the Vietnam War had now become international. It was a major plank in the programme of an organisation calling itself Students for a Democratic Society. When the German branch of the SDS organised a conference in West Berlin on 17 February, thousands of delegates from all over Europe turned up. The following day they led a march of somewhere between 10,000 and 20,000 anti-American demonstrators through the streets of the city.

By March demonstrations had become common-place in US high schools as well as colleges. In a Brooklyn school teenagers took possession of the building and set off fire alarms simply because they did not like school food and wanted the teachers to organise more dances. No wonder the president of Columbia University grumbled: 'I know of no time in our history when the gap between generations has been wider or more potentially dangerous.' And it was global: in places as far apart as Japan and Brazil, Germany and Britain, malcontents wishing to draw attention to their cause learned the lesson of how to attract publicity. In Rome the university was closed for two weeks because of clashes between students and police which had put 200 protes-tors in hospital. A similar situation occurred in Madrid where the university remained closed from late March to early May. In Britain, Cambridge students tried to overturn the car carrying the defence secretary, and their Oxford counterparts, not to be outdone, tried to duck the home secretary in a pond. At Sussex University a visiting American diplomat was sprayed with paint. That these were not mere isolated undergraduate pranks was made abundantly clear on 17 March, when thousands of people marched on the American embassy in London to demonstrate against the Vietnam War. In violent clashes with riot police 91 demonstrators were injured and 200 were arrested.

If word had leaked out of an event that had taken place only the previous day, there is no telling how much more serious things might have become. The 16th of March 1968 was the day of the My Lai massacre. An infantry division in central Vietnam slaughtered more than 500 civilians – men and women, old and young, children and babes in arms. The troops, angered and frustrated by their own losses (more than 500 of their colleagues had been killed in a single week), indulged in an orgy of murder, rape and arson that would forever be a stain on their nation. But not yet. This was one atrocity the military did manage to cover up – for more than eighteen months.

In the comfortable West, respectable society could still deplore demonstrators as 'hooligans', 'pranksters' and 'lefties', but there was a growing recognition that the revolt of international youth was a significant sign of the times, a declaration that young people who were old enough to die for their country were not prepared to have their futures decided for them by a generation who had already been responsible for two major wars in thirty years. It was easy to be critical of the disturbances because these largely unrelated outbreaks of protest activity, although they did not lack leaders with ideals, had no coordination, no common vision of what a 'better world' would look like. When students led by Daniel Cohn-Bendit occupied the administrative offices of the University of Nanterre, Paris, on 22 March, President de Gaulle denounced the mischief-makers as communists and layabouts who wanted to shut down the institution because they could not pass their exams. In fact, the disturbances that disrupted student life in the spring had various elements. Some protestors were agitating against the Vietnam War (the French government was trying to broker a settlement). Some *were* communists. Others were campaigning for more sexual freedom – including mixed dormitories. Simultaneously, Howard University, Washington DC, was brought to a halt by protestors who opposed the draft and the war and wanted more Afro-centric courses. The following week a Brazilian student was shot dead for presuming to demand cheaper student meals.

In the West, demonstrations were an annoyance to the establishment. In eastern Europe they were simply not allowed to happen. The nations of the Eastern Bloc from the Baltic to the Adriatic were controlled from Moscow by the imperial 'Big Brother' of the Soviet government. But, since Stalin's death in 1953, the regime had found it increasingly difficult to contain nationalist and democratic aspirations. By 1968 Yugoslavia and Albania had loosened their ties with Moscow, and other satellites were seeking to express forms of communism less rigidly constrained by the Soviet model. In January Alexander Dubček, a moderate

and a Slovak patriot, became first secretary of the
Czechoslovak Communist Party. He declared his
mission to be the building of 'an advanced socialist
society on sound economic foundations... that
corresponds to the historical democratic traditions
of Czechoslovakia'. Dubček believed that good
communists did not need to isolate themselves from
the capitalist world; rather they should demonstrate that anything the bourgeois West could do
they could do better. Czechoslovak society began
to open up. Press censorship was relaxed. Foreign
travel was permitted. The activities of the secret
police came under tighter control. Even the possibility of multi-party government was accepted. The
effect on the people was electrifying. It is impossible
for a suppressed population to be satisfied with a
little freedom. Once the door is opened a crack it
inevitably gets pushed wider. Encouraged by the
kind of popular protests they could now see taking
place in the West, thanks to new media access, there
was a clamour for more 'rights' and 'freedoms'. This
wave of hope and euphoria was dubbed the 'Prague
Spring'.

On the last day of March President Johnson went
on television and told a shocked nation that he
would not be standing for re-election the following
November. It was an acknowledgement that his
government was so unpopular that the Democratic
Party could not win if he remained at the helm.

The Vietnam War, which many were convinced was unwinnable, was undermining the national economy and America's international standing. The administration was faced with two equally unattractive alternatives: to continue pouring human lives and financial resources into the bottomless pit or to lose face by pulling out. Serious diplomatic moves were afoot to enable the disputants to disengage without losing face but they never got beyond the preliminaries because the two sides could not even agree on a neutral venue for talks. The only crumb of comfort for the Democrats was that Robert Kennedy, charismatic brother of the assassinated John F. Kennedy, announced his intention to run for president.

On 4 April, just when it seemed things could not possibly get much worse for the US government, America was rocked by an atrocity whose effects reverberated around the world. Martin Luther King was steadily becoming yesterday's man as the civil rights movement descended into more and more violence. He was depressed at his failure to reconcile the black and white societies of his native land. But his work continued and in April he was in Memphis, Tennessee, to support striking refuse collectors. On the evening of the 4th he was standing on the balcony of his motel room when a white escaped convict, James Earl Ray, shot him dead. The black power movement could not have hoped for better fortune. They now had a martyr. Forty American cities erupted into bloody mayhem as black mobs went on the rampage, burning and looting shops, overturning vehicles, stoning police and confronting the National Guard. Local authorities met violence with violence. Before the storm had passed scores of people lay dead on the streets. And still the student demonstrations continued. In the last week of the month it was the turn of Columbia University, New York, to be shut down by protestors. By the time police had removed the last students occupying the university buildings ,there had been 700 arrests and 150 serious injuries. In distant places the shock news of King's assassination spawned reactions that had little or no logical connection to the atrocity in Memphis. In Berlin, after days of riots and arson attacks across West Germany, one of the communist agitators, Rudi Dutschke, was shot and very seriously injured by a right-wing vigilante. When interrogated, the would-be assassin explained: 'I heard of the death of Martin Luther King and since I hate communists I felt I must kill Dutschke.'

One fact that now became apparent to commentators was that regimes in power, whatever their political make-up, all responded to challenges in the same way. When Polish students took a leaf from the book of their American counterparts, they had to face police wielding batons and water cannon. A modest demonstration on the campus of Warsaw University provoked the overkill of 500 armed officials being let loose on the offenders. Moscow was nervous about what was happening in Czechoslovakia and determined that Dubček's liberal experiment should not be repeated elsewhere. The reaction of the protestors was also the same on both sides of the Iron Curtain. Within days there were riots on the streets of Cracow, Gdansk and other Polish cities.

As often happens, the industrialised nations, obsessed with their own problems, had little thought to spare for horrors that were ruining millions of lives elsewhere. In 1966 the Nigerian republic fragmented along tribal lines. Massacres and pogroms became the norm of life in several regions. The principal source of revenue came from oilfields located in the eastern regions of Biafra. In July 1967, Biafran leaders, believing that central government was using its wealth to wage ethnic war, declared the region's independence. This escalated the conflict, whose horrors soon made the student—police confrontations in Europe and America look like unfortunate little misunderstandings. By the spring of 1968 what came to be called the Biafran War was in a state of stalemate. The Lagos government, supplied with battlefield weapons and aeroplanes by the Soviet Union, hammered Biafra mercilessly, but was unable to break the rebel state's resistance. The Biafrans, employing bands of European mercenaries, staged several effective counter-attacks. The breakaway region was, in effect, under siege. Lagos decided that if they could not break the enemy militarily it would starve them out.

The worst suffering was inflicted on the ordinary people caught between the armies. When reports began to emerge (and when Western readers were prepared to take an interest), it was clear that a humanitarian disaster of horrifying proportions was unfolding in West Africa. A million Biafrans, driven from their homes by the fighting, were living – and dying – in refugee camps. Starvation and disease were killing thousands every week. For the first time images of skeletal African children appeared on Western TV screens. Humanitarian agencies called on western leaders to intervene in the holocaust but the lesson governments drew from the Vietnam crisis was that getting involved in other people's quarrels was a mug's game. It was left to charitable organisations to try to bring relief to Biafra's people. From the spring the Red Cross and other agencies – some set up specifically to deal with the Biafran crisis – began flying in food and medical supplies. But they could only do so by running dangerous night missions because the Nigerian government deliberately blocked all aid efforts. Adventurous pilots took considerable risks to bring their planes down on improvised landing strips. Nor were they immune from criticism back home. Some people pointed out that by stiffening Biafran resistance they were only delaying the inevitable – at the cost of tens of thousands more lives.

France was still, to use an expressive French word, *mouvementé*. It was on the verge of political collapse. Paris, which had a long tradition of revolution, once again saw its streets blocked by barricades. Students had not ceased mounting protests for their own mixed reasons and now public-sector workers began agitating over their pay and conditions. With talks scheduled to start on the Vietnam issue, members of the international press corps descended on the capital in large numbers. Agitators were not slow to see the importance of this. On 6 May, when the Nanterre student leader, Cohn-Bendit, was summoned to appear before a university disciplinary board, a thousand students turned out to support him. The government took the emergency measure of banning demonstrations. This, of course, had the opposite effect. A swollen crowd of angry protestors raged through the streets and converged on the Sorbonne building in the heart of the old city. Baton-wielding police were confronted by hundreds of men and women shouting, overturning cars to form barricades and tearing up the cobbles to hurl at their assailants. Within a few hours the numbers of injured, on both sides, had reached over a thousand. Over a wide area of Paris the authorities lost control of the streets. The Sorbonne was closed down for the first time in its 700-year history. Day after day, defiant marchers paraded the streets waving red flags and singing revolutionary songs as their spiritual predecessors had in the revolutions of 1789, 1830, 1848 and the Paris Commune of 1871. Then, on 13 May, the leading trade unions called their members out on a general strike. The government teetered. President de Gaulle cut short a visit to Romania but was at a loss to know what action to take on his return. With riots getting daily more out of control and anarchists setting fires in the financial area of the city, there was a vacuum of power in France. The government caved in to the strikers, offering a generous settlement. But the unions, understanding their power, turned it down.

The four-yearly circus that is the US presidential election campaign was, by now, well under way. The main focus of public attention was Robert Kennedy. He was young. He was opposed to the Vietnam War. He had sympathy with some of the issues students were concerned about – though not their methods. He was becoming the darling of television viewers and was rapidly learning how to exploit the medium. There was more than an outside chance that he would win the Democratic Party nomination. On 5 June he was celebrating

his victory in the California primaries. He decided
to leave the Hotel Ambassador in Los Angeles by a
rear exit via the kitchen. There an Arab immigrant
by the name of Shirhan Shirhan shot him dead –
perhaps because he resented Kennedy's pro-Israeli
sentiments. This second assassination delivered
another powerful blow to the national psyche. For
the first time in living memory all enthusiasm for
the presidential campaign evaporated and it became
a lacklustre affair. None of the candidates inspired
great confidence. At a time when the world's leading
superpower desperately needed leadership to pull
it out of the mire of internal divisions, self-doubt
and political apathy, there was no contender who
could convincingly drape himself in the mantle of
national messiah.

It may be that the shock of Kennedy's death had
an impact in France. By the beginning of June the
rioters were beginning to fall prey to their own inco-
herence. Most French people tired of the anarchy
and were worried about the loss of order and security. The tragedy in Los Angeles was an indica-
tion of what could happen when extremists took
the law into their own hands. De Gaulle sensed
the changing mood. He called new elections. The
government came to terms with the strikers. On 17
June the last student sit-in at the Sorbonne came
to an end. In the elections of the following week
leftist parties lost heavily as the people of France

got behind de Gaulle in the interests of restoring stability. It had been a very close thing.

By the time the year's halfway point had been turned, governments the world over were keeping a close watch on their student populations. In Rio de Janeiro potential demonstrators were deterred by the appearance on the streets of tanks and armoured vehicles mounted with machine guns. Some universities in Spain, Italy and Germany were non-operational. Clashes occurred in a number of South American cities. The government in Moscow was particularly nervous. Throughout the summer the Soviet leadership was in dialogue with Alexander Dubček, demanding assurances that he was planning no more reforms. Just as the American administration worried about the domino effect of allowing South Vietnam to go communist, so the Soviet leaders feared that if Czechoslovakia wandered too far from the socialist path other satellites would follow suit. Theirs was not just an ideological concern. In the 'Cold War' era of the 1960s and 1970s Europe was a potential battleground. The North Atlantic Treaty Organisation had several troop division and air bases in western Europe and the Warsaw Pact countries massed their military forces on the other side of the Iron Curtain. Neither side could afford to show weakness or division.

In the early summer Warsaw Pact troops had arrived in Czechoslovakia on 'manoeuvres', but when the war games ended, the tanks and trucks showed no readiness to leave. The military threat remained in the background while politicians from Moscow and Warsaw negotiated. The Soviet leaders were reluctant to be heavy-handed. In 1956 they had ruthlessly suppressed a liberal regime in Hungary. The dissidents had been brought back in line but the diplomatic fallout had been serious and long-lasting. For his part, Dubček was concerned to preserve a degree of national sovereignty while assuring Moscow that Czechoslovakia was still soundly communist. Both sides were conscious of walking on eggshells in the summer of 1968. At the beginning of July the Czechoslovak leader was 'invited' to Moscow for talks. Dubček did something no Eastern Bloc politician had ever done: he declined. When Leonid Brezhnev, the Soviet boss, had recovered, he proposed a meeting in Russia between the entire communist leadership of both states. 'Good idea,' Dubček replied. 'You come here.' They came. On 30 July four days of talks took place at Čierna nad Tisou, close to the Soviet border. Dubček assured Brezhnev that his country would remain loyal and Brezhnev promised that there would be no breach of Czechoslovakia's sovereignty. Next day the foreign troops went home. Peace and brotherhood had, apparently, been secured. An excited nation was suddenly open to the world. Thousands of Czechs and Slovaks travelled to the

West and as many visitors arrived in Czechoslovakia to see at first hand the 'miraculous' transformation taking place in that country.

However, on the night of 20–21 August, 2,000 Warsaw Pact tanks and 200,000 troops crossed the Czechoslovak border. Exactly why the Soviet leader's decision was reversed has never been clear. What is clear is that he covered the decision with diplomatic untruth. He claimed that the action was in response to an appeal from the Czechoslovak Communist bosses to suppress dissident forces threatening the state. Dubček and his colleagues were arrested at gunpoint. Explosive shells silenced the voice of Radio Prague. On the streets angry crowds of young people confronted the tanks. Some tried reasoning with the invading soldiers. Some tried blocking the path of the armoured vehicles. Some threw rocks and petrol bombs. Posters and graffiti appeared on walls: 'Ivan Go Home'; 'Lenin Awake! Brezhnev has gone Mad!' and, perhaps most pointedly of all, 'This is not Vietnam'. Nothing made any impression. The tanks rumbled on, crushing walls, buildings, cars, human bodies – any obstacle that stood in their path. If Brezhnev had hoped that swift action would enable him to seal Czechoslovakia from the outside world, his stratagem failed. Within hours film of the crushed republic was smuggled out and began to appear everywhere.

'This is Czechago, USA' – so ran press headlines the next day. By a remarkable coincidence
the troubles in eastern Europe occurred precisely
at the same time that America was experiencing its
latest outbreak of political unrest. For commentators eager to indicate that parts of the nation
now resembled a police state, it was a comparison
impossible to resist. Two things clashed in Chicago
in August 1968: anti-racist, anti-war protestors and
Mayor Daley. Richard J. Daley had been Mayor of
Chicago for thirteen years and was one of the most
powerful and unscrupulous men in American politics. The magnet that drew him and the protestors
disastrously together was the week-long Democratic
Party convention (23–31 August). Daley wanted
to use the publicity of the event to showcase the
improvements he had made to life in the city.
The demonstrators were intent on disrupting the
convention as much as possible for the benefit of
the media. Up to 10,000 young people gathered in
Lincoln Park, some ('Yippies') proposing to hold
an innocuous youth festival. Daley ordered in a
contingent of 23,000 armed police and National
Guardsmen. He was determined to stand no
nonsense. He would not be like other city chiefs
who had allowed protest to get out of hand. His
instructions to the guardians of law and order were
uncompromising: 'Shoot to kill any arsonist or
anyone with a Molotov cocktail in his hand, because

they're potential murderers, and … shoot to maim or cripple anyone looting.'

The convention became a disaster for the Democrats. Delegates could gain entry to the hall only by negotiating barbed-wire barricades and submitting to searches and security checks. Once inside, they witnessed angry, ill-mannered exchanges between speakers on the platform. Someone accused Daley of 'Gestapo tactics'. His civilised response was: 'Fuck you, you Jew son of a bitch! You lousy motherfucker!' Outside, the press and TV cameras were recording several physically violent confrontations. There were the usual shouted taunts, stone-throwing, scared trigger-happy responses from frightened police and baton charges. So much tear gas was fired into the crowds that an evil-smelling pall hung over much of the city. Scores of innocent bystanders got hurt in the scuffles. And all this happened at the time when TV screens were carrying graphic images of the suppression of free speech in Czechoslovakia. Many viewers concluded that power politics were the same the world over. Those in authority would always use the police to maintain their position and to silence any who challenged them. Another similarity was that, in both situations, the men of blood claimed to be acting in the public interest and actually managed to convince large numbers of their respective populations that that was exactly what they were doing.

The majority always mistrust those who rock the boat – no matter how unpleasant life on board may be. Meanwhile, in one of the worst weeks of the Vietnam War, 1,442 American troops were killed or wounded. No winners emerged from any of the clashes of that over-heated summer – but there were millions of losers.

Over the following weeks the aftermath of August's tragedies worked themselves out. In the communist world there were protests against Moscow's action in Albania, Romania, Hungary and Finland. There was even a small demonstration in Moscow's Red Square. Albania now formally seceded from the Warsaw Pact. In the UN Security Council the invasion of Czechoslovakia was condemned and a resolution was proposed calling for the withdrawal of foreign troops. The USSR simply vetoed it. After brief detention in Moscow, Dubček was allowed to return to Prague, but within months he had been given a new job – as a forestry official. A hardline regime was installed and immediately began undoing the recent reforms. It seemed as though nothing had changed in communist eastern Europe, but for the Soviet system the Prague Spring was the beginning of the end. In America the fiasco of the Chicago convention destroyed the Democrats' chances of retaining the presidency. A handful of demonstrators were indicted on charges of conspiracy and incitement to riot. The verdicts against them were overturned on appeal.

By September sports fans and politicians had their sights fixed on the forthcoming Olympic Games, to be held in Mexico. This regular event, designed to bring together the peoples of the world in peaceful, friendly competition, was causing the organisers grave anxiety. Given the events of the previous few months, it seemed inevitable that publicity seekers would be unable to resist the opportunity to make dramatic protests. The Mexican authorities had already had to make one concession to anti-racist pressure: South Africa had been hitherto banned from competition because of its discriminatory apartheid legislation. Early in 1968 the International Olympic Committee had lifted the ban and provoked an immediate angry reaction. Forty countries threatened to boycott the games. The Mexicans begged the IOC to reconsider its position and South Africa was once more blackballed. Britain was one of the countries which tried not to let politics interfere with sport, but a test case in September broke this resolve. Basil D'Oliveira, a South African mixed-race cricketer who had played in England for several years, was chosen for the national team to play South Africa. The host nation let it be known that his inclusion would not be acceptable. The English players themselves, were divided over the issue, as were many of their fans, but, faced with the prospect of allowing another country to determine the make-up of the English squad (and also receiving strong hints from the government), the British cricketing authorities had no alternative but to cancel the tour.

In Mexico the government was a one-party system. The country was ruled by the PRI, the Institutional Revolutionary Party. They were determined *at all costs* to assure the thousands of visitors who would soon be arriving that their safety and security would be guaranteed and that the games would be conducted in a spirit of peace and goodwill. But, like most governments everywhere in that summer of 1968, they had a student problem. Minor demonstrations occurred in several towns. Protestors aired various grievances, but fundamental to all their concerns was the lack of political freedom. Trade unions, for example, were outlawed. Probably violence would not have escalated had it not been for what was happening in many other parts of the world. Disaffected Mexicans were just as much influenced by what they saw on television as their counterparts in France, Italy or the USA. Unfortunately, the government did not learn from events elsewhere how not to handle civil unrest.

By the beginning of August various student groups had come together in the National Strike Council (CNH) to plan the most effective ways to take full advantage of the golden opportunity fate had handed them. Within a month their demonstrations were attracting tens of thousands of supporters. Inevitably, some of the marchers were government infiltrators. The CNH was careful to ensure that its marches were orderly affairs, so that the government could not claim that it was controlled by communists bent on political revolution. PRI leaders had, accordingly, decided that their most effective strategy would not be to try to stop the rallies, but deliberately to provoke the activists to violence, which the forces of law and order could then 'legitimately' suppress. They turned to the US government and expressed their 'concerns over the security of the Olympic Games'. In response the CIA provided weapons, intelligence and advice on riot control.

The latest mass gathering was planned to take place on 2 October in the Tlatelolco area of Mexico City. Some 10,000 demonstrators gathered in the Plaza de las Tres Culturas to hear speeches from the CNH leadership. The square was an enclosed space bordered on all sides by buildings with only a few narrow streets leading off. These exits were soon blocked by tanks, trucks and soldiers. As the light faded towards sunset, helicopters appeared overhead directing the activities of troops on the ground. At the same time snipers in buildings around the square began firing at the troops. They were plain-clothed members of the presidential guard. The angry and frightened soldiers responded with indiscriminate gunfire and followed this up with house-to-house searches and more murders. The panic-stricken demonstrators, as well as many onlookers, tumbled over each other and over the dead and wounded in their efforts to escape, but every exit from the square was blocked by gun-toting soldiery. The massacre went on all night, trucks carting away the bodies before any members of the press corps could form an estimate of the dimensions of the tragedy.

To say that the reports put out by the government-controlled media were muted would be a gargantuan understatement. The official tally of casualties was twenty or so dead and perhaps eighty to a hundred wounded; the estimates were conveniently vague. One thing the Mexican authorities were crystal clear about was that the students were to blame; it was they who had opened fire on the troops. The truth will never be known because families whose loved ones went missing were too frightened of repercussions to make determined enquiries. Over a thousand Mexicans remained unaccounted for. Some were dead. Some were locked away in prison. Some had fled to guerrilla groups in the hills. Their fate was kept secret for decades – certainly long enough for the nations of the world to remain in ignorance as their athletes gathered to face each other in healthy competition in the Olympic stadia.

Three days after the Tlatelolco massacre a much

more low-key event occurred in Northern Ireland but it was one that was to have appalling and long-lasting consequences. Catholics in Derry went ahead with a planned march in protest against discrimination in jobs and housing by the Protestant-controlled provincial government in Belfast. The demonstration had been banned by the authorities but here, as elsewhere, people with a grievance believed that the time for protest was ripe. And here, as elsewhere, the authorities responded with predictable, disproportionate violence, which went on for three days. This is how the – admittedly biased – *Socialist Worker* reported the events:

> Men were beaten in the testicles. Water cannons drove demonstrators from the area, back into the police lines. In Duke Street two double lines of police with drawn batons boxed in a thousand people and started a systematic and sickening bludgeoning... Fighting spread to the centre of the city during the evening as police beat the people back into the Catholic ghetto... This is not a riot. It is an uprising.

The words were prophetic indeed. The suppression of the Derry march in October 1968 was the beginning of the 'Troubles' which were to dominate British life for more than three decades.

In November America sent yet more combat

troops to Vietnam and hoped that peace talks, staggering along in Paris, might provide them with an exit strategy. In one airborne campaign alone US planes dropped three million tons of bombs. It was well on the way to becoming the worst year for American casualties. Between 1 January and 31 December 1968, 14, 589 soldiers died in a war that the majority of their fellow countrymen no longer believed in. And in Paris the talks proper had not even begun; delegates were still arguing where each of them was to sit and what shape their table should be.

November was the month when Americans finally went to the polls to elect a new president. The choice before them was far from exciting. Two grey, middle-aged men, Hubert Humphrey and Richard Nixon, were competing for their votes. The successful candidate turned out to be Nixon, arguably the worst ever incumbent of the White House. The new president's inauguration the following 20 January is, in the light of history, a fitting postscript to a depressing year. That year had begun with an ironic preface: on 1 January 1968 the United Nations had officially declared the coming twelve months the 'Year of Human Rights'!

Chapter 10

1994

What can the words we use tell us about the people we are? Is it significant that it was only in the twentieth century that we found it necessary to invent the terms 'genocide' and 'ethnic cleansing'? Does that mean that the phenomenon of trying to wipe out whole races of people was something that only appeared at this time? Clearly not; as far back as records go we can read stories of territorial conquest involving the annihilation of one race by another, supposedly superior, race. Where now are the Philistines, that significant military nation that ceased to exist as a recognisable entity in the seventh century BC? What about that great Mediterranean trading nation, the Phoenicians? Wiped out by the consecutive hostility of the Romans and the Vandals. In the first century AD the ancient Britons were eradicated by a mix of slaughter and cultural obliteration. Fugitives from the Roman legions would have recognised the doleful words of an Amerindian chief eighteen centuries later:

> It is cold and we have no blankets. My little children are freezing to death. My people, some of them, have run away to the hills and have no blankets, no food. No one knows where they are, perhaps freezing to death. I want to have time to look for my children and see how many of them I can find. Maybe I can find them among the dead… My heart is sick and sad. I am tired.

So spoke the last chief of the Nez Percé tribe of Idaho. The catalogue is a long one of peoples who have disappeared. They were slaughtered, or forced into slavery, or driven from their homelands, or suffered a process of deliberate cultural obliteration and forced assimilation – or, more often, succumbed to a combination of these fates.

So, if genocide and ethnic cleansing have been such persistent features of human history, why is it that we have only recently got around to providing specific labels to describe them? In the Western world, death-dealing on a monumental scale has come close to us only during the last three generations. Before 1914 our great-grandparents could believe that massacres of biblical proportions were – literally – barbaric; that is to say, they only occurred among savages in 'uncivilised' countries and were indeed proof that those dwelling 'in heathen lands afar' needed the help of missionaries and colonial administrators to develop their humanity. The first half of the twentieth century banished any such smug superiority. The carnage on the Western Front in the First World War evoked the response: 'This must never happen again', but at least then it did only involve armies of combatant troops, not civilians. The Nazi Holocaust, the Stalinist purges, the Second World War mass air raids on civilian targets and the obliteration of Hiroshima and Nagasaki revealed just what 'civilised' nations are still capable of. They provoked a new sensitivity to mass murder and one which was stirred every time modern news media informed us of some fresh horror. In today's global village we have learned not to say: 'Such things could never happen here.' When we learn of Pol Pot's Cambodian 'killing fields' in the 1970s, or the 1992–5 Bosnian War, which claimed over 100,000 lives, we cannot shrug our shoulders and say: 'This is nothing to do with us.' To be truly civilised is to care, and to care is to take appropriate action. It was the lack of appropriate action by world leaders that made the Rwandan genocide of 1994 particularly awful.

The Rwandan genocide was caused, in part, by the colonial rulers of Central Africa. The kingdom of Rwanda-Urundi, lying between Lake Victoria and Lake Tanganyika, was the homeland of two seemingly distinct peoples, the Tutsi and the Hutu. When the Belgians took over control of the area from Germany in 1916, holding Rwanda-Urundi as a trust territory under the League of Nations, they discovered that the Tutsi minority were in a dominant position over the agrarian Hutu. And they happily bought into the theory that they were dealing with two racially distinct tribes. Tutsi legends identified their ancestors with immigrants from the Horn of Africa or adjacent parts of the Middle East. In fact, as modern genetic research has established, the Tutsi and Hutu are both Bantu peoples who have lived in eastern-central Africa for centuries. However, the claims to origins beyond sub-Saharan Africa fitted well with racial prejudices common among the colonial rulers. Because the Tutsi were the ruling elite, it followed, according to the theorists, that they were racially superior; that they were of Caucasian origin. The Belgians claimed to be able to discern facial characteristics distinguishing these 'superior' people from the Hutu 'proletariat', and this informed policy decisions. The Tutsi received better educational facilities and members of the Tutsi aristocracy were employed in administrative posts in preference to the Hutu. This maintenance of a two-class system inevitably created resentment among the majority Hutu.

In 1946 the United Nations took over from the old League and pursued more vigorously the welfare of the indigenous peoples. The Belgian administrators were under obligation to prepare the country for independence, something they believed would take decades to achieve. In the event they were overtaken by the pace of change that was sweeping Africa. Belgian insistence on abolishing the Tutsi monarchy and handing over to a democratically elected government sparked off a Hutu uprising and appalling loss of life. The short-term 'answer' to this tribal conflict seemed to be to split the territory into two parts. Rwanda, with its very large Hutu majority, became a republic, and Burundi, where the imbalance was not so great, retained the monarchy, theoretically, with restricted powers. This constitutional restriction counted for nothing, since the king had the backing of the army with its Tutsi officer corps.

Before their hasty departure, the Belgians had installed constitutions based on Western models, but parliamentary democracy is not a plant that flourishes readily in soils composed of traditional ethnic conflict. In neither country was the government prepared to share power with representatives of its tribal foes. Therefore both newly independent countries lived in a state of turmoil. In Burundi the first free elections in 1965 inevitably produced an assembly with a substantial Hutu majority. The king simply nullified the elections. The following year the monarchy itself was abolished when an army coup established a Tutsi military dictatorship.

In the early days of independence, Tutsi cross-border raids tried to destabilise the Rwanda republic led by President Gregoire Kayibandan. This provoked counter-attacks by Rwandan Hutus. All these conflicts generated a massive refugee problem. Hutus fled from Burundi into Rwanda and the neighbouring Congo. Tutsis sought refuge in Burundi and Uganda. The exiles in Uganda organised themselves into a politico-military party, the Rwandan Patriotic Front (RPF). In 1973 it was the turn of Rwanda to slide down the slippery path into military dictatorship. Kayibanda was over-thrown by Major General Juvenal Habyarimana, who thereafter ruled a one-party state controlled by the National Revolutionary Movement for Development (MRND). Power-seeking rebels and power-holding dictators are equally good at providing progressive-sounding titles for their organisations.

In October 1990 the long-threatened armed conflict erupted in Rwanda. The RPF launched an invasion from Uganda. Civil war continued until August 1993. The well-organised and equipped RPF had the upper hand in fighting, carrying out a very effective guerrilla campaign. From quite an early stage in the conflict the Rwandan government instituted a sinister response. Instead of concentrating all their efforts on the military confrontation, they incited ethnic cleansing. A mock attack on their own capital was intended to stir up fear of a Tutsi uprising. In several places government officials ordered Tutsi villages to be burned and their occupants annihilated. The government also called on France and neighbouring Zaire (now the Democratic Republic of the Congo) for help. It was the presence of foreign troops which balked the RPF of success and induced them, under pressure from the United Nations, to agree to meet with their rivals around the conference table. The result was the Arusha Accords. This placed temporary power in the hands of an interim government, a coalition of five parties, including the RPF. A UN peacekeeping force, under the command of a Canadian officer, Lieutenant-General Romeo Dallaire, was sent to monitor the peaceful transition to stable civilian government. He assessed that he would need 5,000 men to keep the peace and supervise the confiscation of weapons. He was provided with 2,600. Even with ten times that number he would have found it impossible to deal with the crisis that developed.

Among politicians on both sides there were only minorities committed to making the peace process work. The hardliners believed that they could win a continuing war. While the RPF planned an ongoing military offensive, Hutu partisans planned a programme of Tutsi annihilation. The presence of the international force was an inconvenience to the government. While appearing to welcome it, they did their best to undermine it. In January 1994 Dallaire reported back to UN headquarters on the situation in the country. He explained that there had been a long and careful build-up in preparation for an all-out attack on the Tutsi. The government had established bodies of trained militia in every area and brought into the country large quantities of assault rifles, grenades and rocket launchers. The recruits were encouraged to see themselves as patriotic heroes. They were given a fine-sounding name, *Interahamwe*, 'those who fight together'. Every such group had its youth wing, consisting of adolescents and children as young as ten. Just as nice German boys and girls had been turned into fanatical members of the Hitler Youth, so Rwanda's next generation were brainwashed into becoming amoral zombies. All citizens were obliged to carry identity cards specifying their tribal origin. This made it easy to identify victims but also, incidentally, undermined the theory that Hutu and Tutsi were two distinct races with obvious physical distinguishing marks.

Dallaire described the vigorous propaganda campaign that was under way. State-controlled press, radio and television stations had been pouring out, for three or four years, a stream of hysterical disinformation, inciting Hutus to turn on their Tutsi neighbours. Newspaper features and broadcasts were backed up by leaflet distributions. Government propaganda played on all the old resentments: the Tutsi were not real Africans; they were foreign interlopers. They had held the Hutu in subjection for generations. They were bent on regaining their old ascendancy. The only way to prevent this was by a pre-emptive strike. Dallaire gave details of arms caches that had been discovered and described how military experts had been hired to train the Hutu militias. More sinister was a plot he revealed designed to force UN troop withdrawal: an anti-Tutsi demonstration was to be arranged in a place where RPF militants were well established. UN personnel would be present to ensure that the demonstration remained peaceful. The plan was to provoke the RPF into firing on the crowd and killing foreign troops as well as marchers. If the UN soldiers could be tricked into using their weapons in self-defence, government troops would then have an excuse for retaliation, the UN would be discredited and their agents would be pulled out.

The commander of the peacekeeping force indicated his intention of seizing the weapons caches. Back came the reply from UN headquarters that he was to do no such thing. In the distant peaceful environment of the Security Council's chamber in New York, it had been decided that Rwanda was experiencing a civil war and Dallaire's mandate was one of strict non-intervention. He was reminded that he and his men were there simply to keep civilian casualties to a minimum by methods consonant with their own safety and the avoidance of military force. Over the ensuing months, as mass slaughter claimed hundreds of thousands of victims, the foreign troops were rendered powerless not only by the scale of the atrocity, but also by the fact that their orders bore no relation to the situation they were facing.

That situation became suddenly worse on 6 April. An aeroplane carrying the presidents of Rwanda and Burundi was shot down as it approached the airport at Kigali, the Rwandan capital. Both sides blamed each other for the atrocity and the government-backed TV station even accused the UN force of complicity in it. It has never been established beyond doubt just who was responsible for the double assassination but it certainly gave the Hutu leadership the *casus belli* they were looking for. They now had an excuse to unleash a campaign of unrestricted savagery on the entire Tutsi population. What happened over the next three months was not a spontaneous outburst of mob rule; it was not even a campaign that got out of hand; it was the outcome of what had been deliberately planned over the previous three or four years. The rationale behind the policy was that the only way to prevent Tutsis invading

Rwanda and re-establishing their old supremacy was to annihilate every member of the accursed tribe that could be found. The killing of President Habyarimana played right into the government's hands because it could be interpreted as justifying what they had been warning about for the last few years. (There remains a strong suspicion, which may well have substance, that it was Hutu extremists who brought down the presidential plane in order to kick-start the genocide which now followed.)

The outside world, including delegates to the UN, could not understand what was going on. Those who could be bothered to think about it at all perceived it as just another African civil war. There had been several of those since independence as indigenous leaders tried to make European-style representative government work in their very different cultures. A BBC television reporter made the point very succinctly in one of his communiqués in April:

> Look, you have to understand that there are two wars going on here. There's a shooting war and a genocide war. The two are connected but also distinct. In the shooting war there are two conventional armies at each other and in the genocide war one of those armies, the government side with help from civilians, is involved in mass killings.

What was happening was that the more success the RPF had in the field, the more desperate became the Hutu backlash against civilians.

Dallaire and his men were in the eye of the storm and at considerable personal risk. That became very clear the day after the presidential plane crash. The Rwandan army chief, Colonel Bagosora, moved in to take over the government. He sent a force to storm the radio station which was being guarded by UN troops. Dallaire's protest that this was illegal and that, according to the Arusha Accords, the prime minister should take over the presidency in a temporary capacity, was swept aside. In order to make his point, Bagosora ordered the assassination of the prime minister and other moderate politicians. Also killed were ten Belgian soldiers with the peacekeeping force. Their Ghanaian comrades were released. However, by 12 April, the government had been forced to quit Kigali and establish themselves in Gitarama, some fifty kilometres to the south-east. This only made them more determined to continue with their kind of war. They gave a new meaning to the expression, 'scorched earth'. In wars of the past it was a common tactic for retreating armies to leave the land behind them desolate, with no crops or cattle to be commandeered by their pursuing enemies. In Rwanda the country was deliberately stripped of people. If the RPF took over the country they would find themselves without an ethnic power base. That, at least, was the theory behind the strategy employed by the Hutu militants.

The genocide was carried out with a horrifying combination of white-hot hatred and ice cold efficiency. The military put up road blocks and isolated Tutsi communities in order to make the killing process as easy as possible. The government-controlled media was used to provide specific information to the Hutu population about how to find and dispose of their 'enemies'. Listeners were warned that if they did not share in the homicidal frenzy they would share in the fate of the victims. 'Kill or be killed' was the order of the day. Dallaire's contingent were not the only foreigners at risk. Missionaries and aid workers who tried to protect those who sought refuge with them were particularly vulnerable. When trucks of soldiers came roaring into their compounds, they could only watch in horror as doors were smashed and their indigenous colleagues were gunned down alongside any Hutus they were protecting. In one Catholic church scores of children were sprayed with automatic gunfire. Another church sheltering 1,500 Tutsis was bulldozed. Those not crushed were hacked down with machetes as they tried to escape. What made that disaster even more shocking was that the priest of the church assisted in the carnage and was later convicted of crimes against humanity. Such events were daily occurrences and there are hundreds of stories of orchestrated inhumanity that took place during the hundred days that followed the death of the two presidents. Most of the violence, however, was perpetrated on an individual basis. People were hacked or beaten to death with crude or makeshift weapons by their own neighbours, work colleagues, even by their relatives, for special loathing was reserved for those who had dared to intermarry with the 'enemy'.

One depressingly interesting fact that underlines the orchestrated nature of the genocide is that the government was conscious of international opinion. While not for one moment responding to criticism from abroad, Bagasora and his men were concerned that what they were doing should be understood correctly. They genuinely believed that behind the carnage there was some kind of twisted morality. So, when groups of Hutu got out of hand and went on drunken orgies of uncoordinated murder, rape and pillage, they were arrested for sullying the 'pure' motives of the purge. When the world's media arrived with TV cameras and helicopters, word went out to the militias to avoid giving any impression of indiscriminate slaughter. Thus, if a town street or country field was littered with bodies awaiting collection, local leaders were instructed to cover them with banana leaves so that they could not be photographed from the air.

It goes almost without saying that rape figured prominently in the Hutu backlash. When women and girls were rounded up, sexual violence was the rule rather than the exception. One result was the birth of an estimated 5,000 unwanted babies. Those who survived these attacks suffered not only psychological trauma, but, in very many cases, were left HIV positive. Perhaps as many as half a million females were treated in this way. Nor were men and boys immune to this kind of degradation.

Meanwhile, the invaders, now numbering some 25,000, pressed steadily towards the capital in a well-coordinated, three-pronged assault. The Rwandan army, the FAR, was no match for the RPF, who had trained in special camps set up in Uganda. The genocide certainly did not weaken the resolve of the invaders. Quite the reverse; RPF commanders were all the more determined to bring the war to a swift conclusion in order to minimise the civilian murders. On 22 May Tutsi troops captured Kigali Airport. Six weeks of heavy fighting followed around the capital until, on 3 July, the government forces fled. For the RPF it was now just a question of mopping up the last pockets of resistance. The government had already moved on to Gisenyi, on the border with Zaire. When this fell to the RPF on 17 July, the war was over.

But not the killing. As Tutsi civilians returned from hiding or exile the recriminations began. The tables were turned. Before an interim multi-party government could be set up with the power to establish law and order, Hutus were hunted down and butchered as punishment for their part in the recent massacres. Two million did not wait to experience the rough justice exercised on their neighbours. They fled across the border into Zaire, thus creating an enormous refugee problem. In the main refugee camp at Goma, as a result of inadequate water supplies and sanitation arrangements, thousands died of cholera in the next couple of years. The final death toll in the Rwandan genocide will never be known. The UN put the figure of Tutsi and moderate Hutu deaths at 800,000. The new Rwandan government claimed that 1,174,000 men, women and children had perished. Whatever the precise figures might be, the tribal balance had been completely changed and the surviving society was made up in great part of widows and orphans.

What was the rest of the world doing while this tiny country was tearing itself apart? Basically, we did not want to know. When Lieutenant-General Dallaire sent his now-famous 1994 message to his boss at UN headquarters describing the situation, it was not passed on to the Security Council. The man in charge of peacemaking activities at that time was Kofi Annan of Ghana. In 2004 that same Kofi Annan had risen to be secretary-general and, on 7 April of that year, he spoke in Geneva at a meeting marking the tenth anniversary of the genocide. He said:

We must never forget our collective failure to protect at least 800,000 defenceless men, women and children who perished in Rwanda ten years ago. Such crimes cannot be reversed. Such failures cannot be repaired. The dead cannot be brought back to life. So what can we do? First, we must all acknowledge our responsibility for not having done more to prevent or stop the genocide. Neither the United Nations Secretariat, nor the Security Council, nor Member States in general, nor the international media, paid enough attention to the gathering signs of disaster. Still less did we take timely action.

When we recall such events and ask, 'Why did noone intervene?' we should address the question not only to the United Nations, or even to its Member States. No one can claim ignorance. All who were playing any part in world affairs at the time should ask, 'What more could I have done? How would I react next time – and what am I doing now to make it less likely there will be a next time?'

The UN's top man must have been bearing his own burden of guilt when he warned that failure to take action in situations where violence was escalating out of control was 'the beginning of a swift descent into a different moral universe'.

Back in 1994 the UN was hampered by two self-imposed fetters. One was the definition of 'genocide'; the other was the restrictions concerning intervention in the internal affairs of countries. The UN Convention on Genocide was framed in 1948 in the aftermath of the Second World War and the Nazi Holocaust. Its definition of the word was comprehensive:

> ...genocide means any of the following acts committed with intent to destroy, in whole or in part, a national, ethnical, racial or religious group:
>
> (a) Killing members of the group
> (b) Causing serious bodily or mental harm to members of the group
> (c) Deliberately inflicting on the group conditions of life calculated to bring about its physical destruction in whole or in part
> (d) Imposing measures intended to prevent births within the group
> (e) Forcibly transferring children of the group to another group

The convention stipulated that anyone committing genocide, thus defined, 'whether they are constitutionally responsible rulers, public officials or private individuals', were to be 'punished'. But it did not specify what form this punishment would take, nor what body would be responsible for imposing it.

The framers of the UN Charter had walked a tightrope when it came to the relationship between international law and the sovereignty of states. While affirming the responsibility of the Security Council to call upon member states to act to maintain international peace and security, it was careful to insist (Article 2.7): 'Nothing contained in the present Charter should authorise the United Nations to intervene in matters which are essentially within the domestic jurisdiction of any state.'

When the crisis of 1994 came along there was ample opportunity for foot-dragging while diplomats in New York wrangled about whether what was happening in Rwanda was or was not genocide and whether it constituted a purely 'domestic' crisis.

As the bloodshed got under way and as the invading force began their march to Kigali fears, mounted for the safety of foreign diplomats and aid workers. Embassies were closed and staff made for the airport in order to escape while there was still time. Dallaire received new orders: his priority now was not peacekeeping, but the evacuation of foreign nationals. The first direct result of this was the removal of the UN guard on a school where 2,000 Tutsis had taken shelter. A beer-swilling Hutu mob watched gleefully as the soldiers marched out, then went in and gave full rein to their bloodlust. After the shooting of Belgian members of the UN force, Belgium withdrew its entire contingent. Days later the Security Council voted to strip Dallaire of virtually all his men. He was left with just 260 members of the international peacekeeping team. With this pitifully inadequate force he performed wonders. He established and maintained safe areas and brought thousands of Tutsis within them. At the end of May he arranged an exchange of refugees which enabled civilians from both sides to reach safe havens.

But his superiors were intent on avoiding commitment to Rwanda. With the news media revealing the atrocities taking place on a daily basis, the Security Council continued to turn a blind eye. The first Western leader to call a spade a spade (on 27 April) was Pope John Paul II, but his condemnation failed to receive official support in New York. As long as it was remotely possible within the bounds of logic to maintain the fiction that what was happening in Rwanda was not genocide, council members did just that. The USA administration forbade any of its diplomats from using the 'g' word. Not until mid-June did the American secretary of state reluctantly concede that the headline-grabbing slaughter of hundreds of thousands of human beings might be construed as genocide. Even then, this change of heart did not translate into effective action. When the Americans agreed to provide Dallaire with fifty armoured personnel carriers, they took so long about it – and then only delivered them in Uganda – that they reached the peacekeeping force too late to be of much use. When the USA was asked to provide jamming equipment to silence the hate messages being aired by the government radio station, the response was that America could not associate itself with such an infringement of free speech. In 1998 President Clinton came as close as any statesman ever does come to an apology. In a visit to Kigali he acknowledged that 'we in the United States and the world community did not do as much as we could have and should have done to try to limit what occurred'. He regretted that he had not sanctioned the sending of American troops to Rwanda. Britain's UN representative, as usual, followed the American line in 1994 and went even further. When Washington sanctioned the sending of a fact-finding mission to the stricken country, Britain vetoed the proposal in the Security Council.

Was there more behind this snail-pace diplomacy than meets the eye? Were Rwandans as much the victims of big-power politics as of ethnic rivalry? The French government certainly thought so. François Mitterand, the president, in confidential documents released only years later, asserted that Britain and America were involved in a plot to oust the Hutu government and establish a friendly, English-speaking, Tutsi nation. France had a long history of supporting French-speaking governments in Africa, and military advisers had been training Rwandan forces before the outbreak of the 1994 crisis. Now, since the Security Council was floundering in a mire of indecision and inactivity, the French delegation obtained backing for a rescue mission. In late June they set up 'Operation Turquoise'.

This involved the sending of 3,000 troops from France and French ex-colonies, backed by helicopters, warplanes, armed personnel carriers and mortars. The defined objective of Operation Turquoise was:

> …contributing to the security and protection of displaced persons, refugees and civilians in Danger in Rwanda, by means including the establishment and maintenance, where possible, of safe humanitarian areas.

The new arrivals established control of a large area of south-west Rwanda, policed the ending of violence and enabled refugees to leave the country. However, observers called French neutrality in to question. Just as some people believed that Britain and America were hand in glove with the Tutsis, others claimed that French soldiers were still working with the Hutu government. Some accused the French of aiding and even participating in acts of anti-Tutsi genocide. Undoubtedly, the hard-pressed Hutu authorities welcomed the French as 'allies' and spread the word that the foreigners had come to help them in their mission to rid the land of Tutsis. The government radio station was re-established in the safe corridor and continued pumping out its message of hate. The French came under immediate criticism for not putting a stop to such broadcasts and for not arresting Hutu leaders who were killing under the protection of the French flag. The official answer to such complaints was that the peacekeepers were there to save lives and not to investigate accusations of war crimes. Operation Turquoise came to an end (as had been specified in its mandate) on 21 August. The RPF immediately moved in and thousands of Hutus, now unprotected, fled westwards. There is no doubt that the brief French occupation did minimise the killings. The government in Paris could and did claim that France alone among the major powers had exercised compassion and alleviated suffering. But the suspicion of collusion refused to go away. Years later it led to a severing of diplomatic relations between France and the new government of Rwanda.

Did the French have any convincing evidence for suspecting that the anglophone nations had a secret agenda? The career of Paul Kagame was certainly something they could point to. Kagame was a Tutsi military officer living in Uganda in the 1980s. He gave his support to the Ugandan rebel leader, Yoweri Museveni, who succeeded in overthrowing the government of Milton Obote in 1985. Kagame joined Museveni's cabinet as a minister responsible for military intelligence. The following year Kagame became a co-founder of the RPF. He had, thus, emerged as an important figure in eastern Central Africa. In 1990, with Rwanda rapidly becoming more unstable, Kagame was invited to America, where he received military training at Fort Leavenworth, one of the US Army's most prestigious bases. Known as the 'intellectual centre' of the army, Leavenworth majors on military ideology and has a specialist Foreign Military Studies Office. This connection led to both the USA and Britain providing the RPF with training and equipment. On the assassination of his friend and RPF co-founder, Kagame returned to Uganda to take over sole leadership of the organisation. Kagame's prestige and power were enormously enhanced by the RPF's success in 1994 and his upward mobility took him to the Rwandan presidency in 2000.

With his Ugandan allies, Kagame was allegedly involved in civil war in the neighbouring Congo state (formerly Zaire). This provoked vociferous condemnation, led by France. Kagame was accused of crimes against humanity and of looting in the mineral-rich areas of Congo. Charges extended to Kagame's earlier career. He was said to have organised anti-Hutu genocide and, specifically, to have been personally responsible for the downing of the presidential aeroplane. Noone had ever been indicted for that crime and this provoked accusations of cover-up.

> It defies logic why the UN Security Council has never mandated an investigation of this missile attack to establish who was responsible, especially as everyone agrees it was the one incident that touched off... the 'Rwanda genocide'.

So wrote one Rwandan commentator and he was not alone in airing conspiracy theories. In 2001 Amnesty International added its voice to the growing choir of those who insisted that the RPF was as guilty of genocide as the Hutu government. As we have seen, growing ill-will between France and the Kagame regime led to the severing of diplomatic relations in 2006.

It is clear that Kagame was a protégé of the current USA administration in 1994 and, to a lesser extent, of the Conservative government in Britain. There were – officially – no anglophone military personnel in Uganda or Rwanda during the civil war. Certainly, Kagame's foreign friends could not be seen to be directly involved but there are more ways to skin a rabbit and the delaying tactics of America and Britain at UN headquarters allowed the RPF to gain military dominance, which translated into political control in the aftermath of the

war. If this was deliberate policy, then both governments stand condemned of complicity in one of
the most appalling examples of genocide in modern
history.

Wherever there is political instability in the
'global village', world leaders are bound to weigh
carefully the pros and cons of intervention.
National self-interest comes at the top of the list
and, perhaps, rightly so. It is reasonable to consider
the political returns of any military action that will
involve spending taxpayers' money and risking the
lives of service personnel. But there must come a
point where humanitarian considerations count for
more than national advantage. In the early 1990s
Rwanda was the most densely populated country
in the whole of Africa and the competition for agricultural land was one of the main reasons for ethnic
rivalry. It was a situation to which there could be no
short-term solution. Rwanda also stood on the line
dividing English-speaking from French-speaking
Africa. Ex-colonial nations no longer used the
nineteenth-century term 'spheres of influence', but
it was inevitable that France and Belgium on one
hand and Britain and the USA on the other should
take a proprietorial interest in Rwanda and the best
ways of achieving its stability. In 1994 the franco-
phone nations backed the government which represented the Hutu majority. They responded to the
call of the *de jure* administration for help in resisting

invasion from across their border. The partners in the 'special relationship' backed the better-educated Tutsis, who were also important because of their friendship with Uganda. Given this alignment and given also the fact that Rwanda's population – both Hutu and Tutsi – had little significance in the grand scheme of things, the major Western powers felt no urgency about intervening. Belgium was, after the killing of its soldiers, at one with Britain and America in maintaining a hands-off stance. As the genocide got under way, and as the RPF was seen to be winning the war, there was little incentive for greater involvement by the major Security Council members. France was more inclined to intervene but embarrassed by the bad press the Hutus were gaining – hence its very belated initiative.

No one emerged from the Rwandan genocide with clean hands. Power-seeking indigenous politicians had their own agendas. It was easy in a land where tribal conflict had a long history to whip up ethnic hatred and encourage all manner of bestiality. French and Anglo-American prestige was certainly tangled up in the crisis. Many Western diplomats and statesmen were more concerned about their own standing in Africa than about the fate of millions of Tutsi and Hutu victims who lived in a distant country and with whom they could not identify. Perhaps we ought to question very seriously that 'global village' cliché. Almost 400 years

ago, John Donne affirmed: 'Any man's death dimin-
ishes me, because I am involved in *Mankind*.' Are
we yet ready to embrace that philosophy?